THE AUTISM FULL EMPLOYMENT ACT

The Next Stage of Jobs for Adults with Autism, ADHD, and Other Learning and Mental Health Differences

MICHAEL BERNICK
AND LOUIS A. VISMARA, MD

Skyhorse Publishing

Skyhorse Publishing books may be purchased in bulk at special discounts for sales promotion, corporate gifts, fund-raising, or educational purposes. Special editions can also be created to specifications. For details, contact the Special Sales Department, Skyhorse Publishing, 307 West 36th Street, 11th Floor, New York, NY 10018 or info@skyhorsepublishing.com.

Skyhorse® and Skyhorse Publishing® are registered trademarks of Skyhorse Publishing, Inc.®, a Delaware corporation.

Visit our website at www.skyhorsepublishing.com.

10 9 8 7 6 5 4 3 2 1

Library of Congress Cataloging-in-Publication Data is available on file.

Cover design by Kai Texel

Print ISBN: 978-1-5107-6732-4
Ebook ISBN: 978-1-5107-6733-1

Printed in the United States of America

CONTENTS

Once again, for Donna
—msb

To Wendy & Mark, for their profound love & support
—lav

INTRODUCTION

HOW WE CAME TO THIS ACT

Employment remains *the* issue today for our adult autism group of Northern California, AASCEND (the Autism Aspergers Spectrum Coalition for Education Networking and Development), just as it has been since the start of AASCEND in 1999. Housing, mental health services, and police relations are all concerns, but none holds the same importance as employment to our members.

So it came to be in the pandemic summer of 2020 that we set out to develop an Autism Full Employment Act. At the time, the national economy (especially the California economy) was decimated, and it was clear that it would need to be rebuilt, starting in 2021 and beyond. The Act would be an attempt not only to rebuild autism employment programs, but also to address the limitations and shortcomings of the current system.

In developing employment strategies for the Act, we drew on our AASCEND experiences. We drew on the experiences of other autism groups and practitioners throughout the United States: the state vocational rehabilitation programs and the departments of developmental disabilities, the autism employment initiatives and autism consultancies, and the autism-focused businesses.

The strategies set out in this volume are meant as a starting point, a framework. The details of these strategies remain to be filled in as the Act is developed. The details will be a collective effort: adults with autism joining with family members and advocates. When we started our efforts, we thought of a single Act. An Act may be the vehicle for these strategies, or it may be that the strategies are pursued through multiple legislative or administrative actions.

In late August 2020, we published a short article in *Forbes* that introduced the concept of the Autism Full Employment Act, and heard from people in the autism community throughout the country who wanted to join the effort. This was not surprising; interest in and commitment to developing a better system of autism employment exist far beyond our AASCEND group.

***

THOUGH WE SPEAK of an Autism Full Employment Act, autism in the Act's title is best understood as a shorthand and proxy. It is shorthand for a range of other developmental and learning differences that have made steady employment difficult for adults. It is also shorthand for a range of mental health conditions that undermine employment. The strategies set out in this volume are intended to include workers with any of these conditions. Throughout much of this volume reference is made to "workers with autism" or "workers with autism and other developmental differences." These terms are meant to refer to the broader group of workers.

At a few points in this volume, reference is made to "workers with disabilities." At AASCEND we do not use this term, as it emphasizes limitations rather than strengths. But it is the term used by the Bureau of Labor Statistics and by most federal, state, and local governments. We use it, albeit reluctantly, when referring to certain government data and program titles.

***

HERE IS A word on my background and the background of Dr. Vismara. My involvement in the employment field started in fall 1979, with a community job training group, the San Francisco Renaissance Center, located in San Francisco's Mission District, and it has continued over the past forty-one years. During the past decade, I've been a volunteer job coach and job developer for adults with autism, facilitator of our AASCEND Autism Job Club, and advisor on individual autism employment programs.

In 2015, I published (with Richard Holden) *The Autism Job Club*, which chronicled the emerging autism employment efforts, in the context of America's shifting job markets and job structures. Since 2016, I've been researching a follow up project, *The Autism City*, a broader look at the autism community in the year 2030, envisioning new housing, public safety, and mental health structures, as well as employment structures. This volume draws on research undertaken as part of that project, and the envisioned employment future.

Dr. Vismara and I have been partners on autism employment projects for more than twenty years, meeting in 1999 when we were both in state government. Dr. Vismara ("Dr. Lou" as he's known in Sacramento) was a prominent cardiologist in California for several decades, before retiring in the mid-1990s to work full time on autism advocacy and programs. He was the autism expert for the California legislature for fifteen years, and the prime mover behind the California Legislative Blue Ribbon Commission on Autism, which led to expanded insurance coverage for autism interventions. He co-founded the University of California Davis Medical Investigation of Neurodevelopmental Disorders (MIND) Institute, now recognized worldwide for its research on the neurobiology of autism.

In Chapter 13 he discusses the employment journey of his son Mark, a man with more severe autism, and in Chapter 14 he analyzes comorbidities. All of the chapters, though, reflect our collaboration, and grow out of ideas we have discussed over the past two decades.

***

THE VARIED STRATEGIES in this volume are rooted in two broad employment policy lessons of the past forty years.

The first is that policy best arises from local experience. In May 1979, thinking of a career in the employment field, I went to see Bill Spring, President Carter's advisor on job training. I hoped I might get a position with him in the White House. Instead, he told me: "Get out of Washington, DC, go work on a local level, gain local experience." I departed Washington, DC, that month, and since have lived and worked on a local level. I now give Bill Spring's advice to young people who want to do something in the employment field. My hope is that young people who want to make a contribution to autism employment will become involved with specific local projects and job seekers. I am happy to say that most are doing so, and you will meet some of them in the following pages.

The second lesson is related to the first: avoid theorizing, as what counts is the end goal of job placement and retention. For five years in the late 1990s and early 2000s, I was director of our state labor department in California, the Employment Development Department. Among the regular refrains then (and now) was that we needed more "coordination of services" or "ending silos" or some other empty system building theory. When the discussion took such a turn, one of our deputy directors, Michael Krisman, would interrupt and say, "What does this mean for the job seeker in Glendale?" That became our mantra for all meetings and proposals.

At one point in *The Adventures of Huckleberry Finn* by Mark Twain, Jim is locked in a shed on the Phelps' farm. Huck sets out to steal the keys to the shed, unlock the door, and free Jim. But Tom says it can't be that simple; they need a hidden tunnel, stolen digging tools, secret messages, and a rope ladder, just as in the adventure books he's read. A good deal of confusion ensues, including Tom being shot and saved only by Jim's heroism, and Jim nearly being sent back into slavery until Aunt Polly arrives and reveals he is a free man.

In autism employment, we don't need to overcomplicate with too many meetings or theories. Often, we just need to get the keys and open the shed door.

***

SIX BROAD STRATEGY areas are set out in the next pages. Interspersed with chapters on these six strategy areas are notes on related issues of "autism talent advantage," "the autism friendly workplace," "professionalizing the direct support workforce," "transitions," and "comorbidities." In the final chapter, we consider why no government action or program can replace the employment journey of each adult with autism, but how instead the Act can hasten these journeys.

THE AUTISM FULL EMPLOYMENT ACT: AN OVERVIEW

The pandemic halts autism employment initiatives, but the upcoming federal recovery efforts provide opportunity to restart and move to the next stages of autism employment. The Act's main strategies are set out, as are the deeper challenges that accompany these strategies.

Part I: The Recovery and the Next Stages of Autism Employment
Within a few months in spring 2020, the COVID-19 pandemic devastated the American job base and economy, and this devastation continued through the summer, fall, and winter as the economic lockdowns by states were extended. The economic recovery beginning in 2021 and continuing over the next few years will not be a quick rebuilding of the job base. But the recovery can improve several areas of employment in America, one of which is autism employment. The recovery can bring a better system of autism employment—if the autism community can come forward with ideas for such a system and the ability to pursue these ideas.

The Autism Full Employment Act is intended to be part of the recovery. The Act sets out a vision for employment of adults with autism and a set of strategies for achieving this vision. It mixes strategies of extra-governmental and mutual support by the autism community itself, with funding strategies for hiring and retention. It includes employment for adults with a wide range of skills and aptitudes.

Over the past decade, autism employment initiatives have multiplied and developed in sophistication across the country. "Autism at Work" programs at major companies have grown in number and participants beyond the early adapters. So too have the past few years seen the growth of both the autism workforce consultancies, partnering with employers in recruitment and retention, and the autism-focused businesses, dedicated to hiring directly adults with autism.

The pandemic halted or slowed most of these efforts. Hiring among the "Autism at Work" programs came to a standstill in March 2020, as did much hiring through the consultancies. The autism-focused businesses struggled to hold on to the program participants they had.

As the overall economy restarts in 2021 and beyond, these autism employment initiatives will restart also. But restarting should not be the end goal. Even in the halcyon economic times before the pandemic, these initiatives reached a small percentage of adults with autism; and even those adults they reached usually had a very precarious hold on their jobs.

The post-pandemic rebuilding offers the chance for building on and refining the effective hiring and retention initiatives that have been undertaken, and developing new ones in the private sector, especially in universities, foundations, and large nonprofits. It offers the chance to open hiring more widely in state and local governments—which have urged private employers to hire adults with autism, but have done little in their own workforces.

Further, it offers the chance to achieve other goals: designing fuller employment for adults with autism who are the more severely impacted, experimenting with new forms of public service employment, expanding the mutual support networks for job search and support, and developing a new cadre of autism employment practitioners.

The autism employment efforts of recent years have tapped into an enormous wellspring of energy and desire to work among adults with autism, family members, and advocates. The post pandemic efforts will similarly need this participation.

Part II: The Main Elements of the Autism Full Employment Act

There is no one strategy, no big idea, no "hedgehog" that will make for a better autism employment system. Rather there are a number of strategies.

Some of the strategies in the Act will be ones that require government action or funding—such as the growth of the autism workforce consultancies and autism-focused businesses and autism hiring in state and local governments. However, others—the autism job clubs, the autism advocacy within companies, and "autism friendly" workplace culture—are included to raise the profile of these strategies, and do not require government investment. The Act will have a hortatory function, in pointing to important mutual support and self-help approaches, and workplace shifts.

The introduction of the strategies in this chapter and discussions in the following chapters are a framework. The details of each of the strategies—the forms of, say, the incentives for private employers, or the expansion of the mutual support activities—remain to be filled in by persons in the autism community joining together, and in partnership with private employers and other hiring entities. Not one of us in the autism community, individually, has the breadth of experience and knowledge to design legislation. It is only by pooling experiences and expertise that we can do so.

Six broad strategy categories stand out from autism employment experiences of the past few decades.

1. Expanding hiring initiatives in private firms, large and small

The past decade has seen an explosion of autism employment initiatives in the private sector, including with some of America's largest employers. The next system will continue to be based in the private sector, building on the effective structures that exist.

The "Autism at Work" initiative is the best known of the private sector autism employment programs. Since the first "Autism at Work" program was launched by the worldwide software firm SAP in 2013, the initiative has expanded to twenty of the largest companies in the United States, including Microsoft, JPMorgan Chase, and EY. The initiative has succeeded in hiring and in developing new structures for retention.

At the same time, the number of direct hires among the "Autism at Work" firms is modest after seven years, totaling fewer than eight hundred by mid-2020. Further, most of the hires are adults with autism who have sophisticated software engineering, coding, or other tech-related skills, and the hiring processes are very competitive.

Beyond "Autism at Work" are other initiatives in private sector hiring. These initiatives are pushed forward by the new autism workforce consultancies, and by the autism employment research and implementation centers that have sprung up across the country, at Cornell, UCLA, Drexel, UC Davis, and Stanford. The largest number of placements continues to be done by the established disability employment providers, such as Goodwill and The Arc. But all of these efforts taken together represent a small segment of adults with autism. The providers all report their job candidates today far outnumber the openings, and each placement is a struggle.

Expanding autism employment in private firms will start with the inter-employer and intra-employer networks. Employers reaching out to other employers has been the most effective means of marketing targeted employment projects from the job training programs of the 1960s to the present. Employers currently involved in autism employment initiatives will be persuasive advocates today—especially as these employers achieve and document placements and retention, and can be transparent about difficulties encountered.

Family members and friends have been important advocates within their companies for autism initiatives, utilizing intra-employer networks. The autism initiatives at SAP, Microsoft, Hewlett Packard, Enterprise, and many lesser-profile companies were the result of family members within these companies pushing the company leadership to start these initiatives.

Beyond these networks, a structure for expansion lies in the emerging subindustry of autism workforce consultancies, such as Integrate, Next for Autism, Uptimize, and EvoLibri, that the Act should look to invest in. These consultancies offer promise for expanding structured autism initiatives in large firms, and to an even greater extent in midsize and small businesses.

The current consultancies are providing customized recruiting, hiring, job coaching and counseling, and showing positive outcomes. They are staffed for the most part by professionals in the autism employment field, who come from backgrounds in business. They are able to aggregate expertise and costs among firms.

The subindustry of consultancies is a modest one at present, with limited financial resources. But with some government investment, it could grow. It could engage the midsize and small businesses that do not have the resources for structured initiatives, and have largely been absent from autism employment initiatives.

2. Expanding employment in universities, foundations, and major nonprofits

Universities have been notably absent as participants in autism employment initiatives. So too have private foundations and large nonprofits been absent. This is so even though these institutions often have greater flexibility and more relaxed work environments than other private sector firms, and even though they often congratulate themselves on their diversity and social goals.

These institutions should be the target of advocacy efforts by employees within who are autism advocates, as well as advocates outside. Universities that receive millions of dollars in autism research funds and non-profits that receive millions of dollars in social services

5

funds should be called on to be consistent with their missions in their own hiring processes.

3. The Autism Job Clubs and mutual support

The Autism Job Clubs are a major form of mutual support: adults with autism and family members and advocates coming together to help each other with job leads, advice, and encouragement. The Act may include modest funding for their replication across the nation. Mainly, though, the Act will highlight their importance—the roles of adults with autism and family members joining together outside of government—and identify the elements that make for an effective Job Club.

4. Local and state governments have urged private employers to hire adults with autism, but have not done so in their own workforces.

Local and state governments have encouraged private sector employers to hire adults with autism and other developmental differences, but have not hired these adults in their own workforces, on any scale. Twenty-two state governments have taken actions under the State as Model Employer program for workers with disabilities, but a good number of these actions have been actions of process, not results.

Results will come through putting in place some of the same models of retention and support and workplace culture that have been developed in the private sector. Results also may come through setting goals specifically for workers with developmental differences, with enforcement mechanisms.

5. Autism-focused businesses, with the specific mission of hiring adults with autism, are now in a range of tech and non-tech fields. These businesses occupy a small, but important, hiring niche.

Ultranauts, Ventures ATL, Extraordinary Ventures, Spectrum Designs, and Daivergent are a few of the autism-focused businesses, with others being established on a regular basis. They are filling a hiring niche, particularly for adults who are not finding jobs in mainstream employment. Their growth lies in investment and support within the autism community and by connecting to the contracting, capital access, and wage subsidies of the broader social enterprise movement.

6. The next system will give more attention to employment for the more severely impacted, including integrated employment and subsidized employment in public service positions.

The majority of the autism employment initiatives in recent years have focused on adults with autism who have advanced skills. The next system will give more attention to employment for the more severely impacted including: new forms of congregate employment, more fully subsidized integrated employment, and subsidized forms of public service employment.

Part III: Jacob Wrestling with the Angel

In developing these six strategies, we must be able to go beyond much of the conventional wisdom and common discussion of autism employment. As in the biblical story of Jacob wrestling with the Angel, we must wrestle with rarely acknowledged and uncomfortable truths. The notes interspersed in this volume raise some of the challenges to be addressed.

"Autism talent advantage": Autism talent advantage is a common phrase among advocates, usually associated with technical skills or memory skills, or some other forms of savant skills. But we're finding that the technical skills are present in only a small segment of the adult autism population, and memory and savant skills are not easily fit into the job market. If we are able to look deeper, though, we will find other skills and characteristics that are truer job advantages.

"Autism friendly" workplace: Similarly, "autism friendly" workplace is included in many of the advocate manuals on autism employment, referencing lighting, sound modifications, or quiet spaces. But these

physical improvements rarely go to the core obstacles for successful employment. The true "autism friendly" workplace will be one with a culture, distinct from most workplaces today, that balances business needs with forms of flexibility and patience.

"Professionalizing" the direct support workforce: The direct support workforce—the job coaches, job counselors, and independent living coaches—provide the front lines of employment programs. As one long time disability services administrator noted in a recent California state legislative hearing, "All our grand plans for service design, quality assurance, monitoring, and accountability do not amount to a 'hill of beans' if the relationship between the direct support professional and the individuals receiving the support is not a quality relationship that can be sustained, consistent over time."[1]

Yet, the current direct support workforce is characterized by high turnover, uneven training, and little cohesion as a profession or craft. "Professionalizing" this workforce needs to get far more attention. One element of this "professionalizing" will include salary levels, but money is only one part. There is a new level of training and commitment that should accompany any salary increases.

Falling off the Cliff and Transition: Just among youth with a diagnosis of autism, an estimated 750,000–1,000,000 will turn eighteen over the next decade. "Falling off the cliff" is the term often used by worried family members and advocates, as the wide range of educational and behavioral services provided by local school districts can end abruptly at eighteen. In fact, the resources for "transition," often free of cost, are considerable. In designing a better autism employment system, we need to look at why these resources are not being accessed, and whether these resources are the most effective.

Comorbidities and Mental Health Conditions: Perhaps most importantly, we need to confront the powerful mental health comorbidities that undermine employment. Such comorbidities as obsessive compulsive disorder, anxiety disorder, and major depressive disorder have neurological ties to autism. They bring impediments to job success that are far more serious than failure to make eye contact or understand social cues.

***

THESE ARE SOME of the deeper challenges to wrestle with as we build a better autism employment system. There are others connected to advocating for additional government roles or funding.

Any advocacy must look hard into the performance of previous employment funding for adults with developmental differences and be willing to acknowledge shortcomings. In my first years with job training and anti-poverty programs (in the early 1980s), the lack of introspection among advocates stood out. Any criticism of the federal anti-poverty programs was met by advocates with "We didn't spend enough money." It was easy to see that this was not accurate, that the programs often suffered operational and conceptual deficiencies. Over time, anti-poverty advocates lost credibility with their unwillingness to be honest about shortcomings.

Along the same lines, autism employment advocacy cannot take for granted the case for additional resources. This case must be made, recognizing the many competing groups. Federal, state, and local officials are inundated with calls for other projects connected to employment, and other targeted employment groups. What claim do we in the autism community have on additional employment resources?

In the next chapter, we start with the autism employment vision on which the Act is built. We consider the meaning of "full employment" in terms of workers with developmental differences, and this meaning in the context of the concerns about a coming shortage of jobs due to automation and technology.

NOTE

1. Eric Zigman, "Panel Remarks for California Senate Subcomittee 3: Provider Rate Study and New Rate Setting Methodology," Sacramento, May 9 2019.

2

THE ACT AND EMPLOYMENT IN THE LIVES OF ADULTS WITH AUTISM

The Act sets out a vision of employment for the range of adults with autism. This vision is discussed, as is the meaning of "Full Employment" in the title of the Act and the relation of the Act to concerns that automation and technology are leading to a shortage of jobs across the economy.

Part I: The Meaning of "A Place in the Job Market"

A place in the job market for all adults with autism who want to work: this is the vision that the Act is built on. The vision includes people with college degrees and those who have not completed high school, people who have an active network of family support and those without, and people with comorbidities and mental health conditions that have been obstacles to jobs.

The relation of the autism community to paid work is at times a complicated one. A significant number of adults with autism receive Supplemental Security Income (SSI) benefits, which include a monthly amount (roughly around $783 monthly) as well as health benefits. They, and especially their family members, are often reluctant to risk the loss of SSI upon going to work.

The federal government has made several attempts in the past two decades to encourage employment by allowing SSI recipients to work and maintain a part of their income. The current system allows SSI recipients to keep a portion of their SSI cash benefit, even as they are employed, and to keep their health benefits for at least a period of time.[1] Despite this more flexible structure, many families fear any change or disruption in SSI benefits. They have gone through considerable paperwork, forms, phone call holds, and appeals to get on SSI, and don't want to take the chance of having to go through the process again. They are correct: dealing with the SSI bureaucracy or related bureaucracy of Social Security Disability Insurance (SSDI) is maddening. Better SSI and SSDI structures remain to be built.

But among the adults who are not on SSI (and even among many who are), by a large majority they say they want to be part of the job world. Surveys and focus groups of adults with autism find they and their families do not have ambivalence about jobs. They want to work for the same reasons as other workers: a role in the economy, income, and a place to go to outside of the house each day. The community agencies providing services to adults with autism report similar findings.

During the pandemic in 2020, our AASCEND Autism Job Club halted operations in March, and reopened only in late June. By that time, most of our members had been laid off, furloughed, or given limited hours.

When we had our June meeting, members talked about how much they wanted to return to their workplaces. Adults with autism are often described as not being social, as desiring solitude. But nearly all members said what they missed most was getting out of the house and having a workplace to go to. Everyone agreed they were "zoomed out," tired of online connections, wanting to return to the life structure of a job.

Dr. Bryna Siegel is one of the pioneers of autism studies who has been providing services and therapy to youth and adults with autism since 1972. In her most recent book, *The Politics of Autism*, she questions the role of parents and other family members in pushing youth with autism to pursue education and work paths that may not be realistic or in the youth's best interest. Siegel argues that youth with mild/moderate autism are too often being directed by parents into college tracks and college, only to drop out. Many would be better off pursuing vocational tracks in high school. Other youth with moderate to severe autism would fare better in informal work arrangements with relatives (helping in a family landscaping business or retail business).

Siegel challenges us to think more fully about the employment strategies undertaken. But Siegel also is clear in her therapy and writing on the importance of employment and purposeful activity.

Our AASCEND adult autism group has workgroups on autism housing, police relations, and health care, as well as employment. By far, employment gets the greatest interest and participation.

David Platzer, an anthropologist, is one of our AASCEND board members who has a brother with autism who is in his thirties. A few years ago he wrote about his brother in a summary worth quoting at length:

> My brother is currently looking for work as a life guard, but his last job was nearly a decade ago. He has an incredible way of looking at the world and a lot to offer everyone he meets. But he also has problems with attention, anxiety, and other things that make productivity hard for him. He struggles with social cues, and, like (Temple) Grandin, describes human behavior as a little bit mysterious. To be blunt, people sometimes find him odd. And so most jobs he has had have not lasted for more than a few months at most. He is also isolated socially, though he would very much like a less lonely existence. He may not bring a competitive advantage as the term is commonly used, but it's hard not to see some role in the job market as good for him and good for the broader society.[2]

The brother's desire for work and the difficulties he's encountered will be familiar to many of us in the autism community—adults with autism and family members.

Part II: The Meaning of "Full Employment" and the Dearth of Data on Autism Employment

The Autism Full Employment Act refers to "Full Employment." A word is in order on the historical uses of this term in federal legislation, and its meaning in the context of autism employment.

Other federal legislative proposals in the post-World War II period have spoken of "full employment," including two that were enacted: The Employment Act of 1946 and the Full Employment and Balanced Growth Act of 1978. Both served mainly to set out "full employment" as a goal. They referenced fiscal and job creation policies that the government might use—though they did not mandate any policies.

The Employment Act of 1946 reflected the widespread Keynesian view of the time: America needed to embrace active fiscal policies, and even direct job creation, to keep unemployment low. The memory of the Great Depression was strong. The previous year, a Full Employment Act of 1945 had declared that "all Americans . . . are entitled to an opportunity for useful, remunerative, regular and full-time employment" and charged the federal government with providing "such volume of Federal investment and expenditure as may be needed." The 1945 Act failed to pass, but did give rise to the 1946 Act that set out a goal of full employment, while requiring it be balanced with other economic goals, particularly price stability and the limiting of the inflation rate.[3]

For the next thirty years following the 1946 Act, unemployment nationally remained low. When it began to climb in the mid-1970s, Senator Hubert Humphrey returned to the idea of full employment legislation. With Representative Augustus Hawkins, Humphrey introduced legislation in 1976 that, two years later, became the Full Employment and Balanced Growth Act of 1978 (known also as the Humphrey Hawkins Full Employment Act). This time a specific target of full employment was set out as no more than a 3 percent unemployment rate for people twenty years or older.

The original legislation set specific strategies to achieve this goal, including the use of public sector job creation (termed "reservoirs of public employment") and aggressive rates of government spending. In the final legislation, though, the strategies were cast as options, but not required. The Act also announced that primary reliance for reducing unemployment would be on private sector initiatives. In the years since 1978, no major "full employment" Act has been passed.

The Autism Full Employment Act does not set a specific unemployment rate to be enforced or even aimed at. It uses the term "full employment" as an aspirational goal for all adults with autism who want to work.

A main reason for this is that we know little on the current status of employment among adults with autism. Researchers at Drexel University's Autism Institute have been among the most active in trying to quantify autism employment rates. In 2017, Drexel published its latest "National Autism Indicators Report" based on a survey of 3,520 working age adults with autism, eighteen to sixty-four years of age. The survey, which attracted wide attention in the autism community, reported that only 14 percent of the adults held a job for pay in the community. The remainder were either in unpaid activity (54 percent) or in no work or day activities (27 percent).[4]

The survey has been widely cited. However, it has a big limitation. It only includes adults accessing services from a state Developmental Disability department. It is skewed to those more severely impacted.

Autism Speaks, the leading national group on autism services, has shied away from specific numbers, but notes on its website that unemployment and underemployment among adults could be as high as 85 percent.[5] This estimate of unemployment and underemployment has been taken up by other websites and other recent articles on autism employment—even though the data sources for this estimate are unclear, as is the meaning of "underemployed." [6]

The Act will seek to fill the research gap. It will set a research path for helping us to understand how autism employment and unemployment differ among segments of the autism community, and how employment and unemployment shift over a work lifetime. It will help us better define a realistic "full employment" rate for adults with autism and other developmental disabilities.

Part III: Boosting Autism Employment among Concerns that America Will Not Have Enough Jobs

In several ways, the Act and its emphasis on employment run against the movement nationally in recent years to de-emphasize work and decouple work from benefits. The Universal Basic Income (UBI) campaign is the most high profile component of this movement. UBI builds on "future of work" warnings that technology and artificial intelligence are eliminating jobs at a rapid pace. This job elimination, it is said, will lead to a deficit of jobs in the near future, necessitating new forms of income support not tied to jobs. UBI urges us to move away from thinking of employment as a central economic organizing principle.

In structuring the Act, we will want to be aware of these concerns. But they should not slow down our efforts. The history of the post-World War II period is filled with warnings about job deficits due to automation or technology that never materialized. Jobs were eliminated by automation/technology, but a greater number of jobs came to be created.

In the early 1960s, for example, the national government and state governments feared that automation was rapidly eliminating jobs, so that unemployment would permanently be above 10 or 15 percent in the United States. In California, the state legislature created the Commission on Manpower, Automation, and Technology, which traveled throughout the state in 1964 gathering testimonies from labor researchers, employers and worker representatives. Much of this testimony came from union officials describing how automation was putting their members out of jobs.[7]

Rather than lose jobs, though, the California economy saw unprecedented job growth in the last half of the 1960s. Automation eliminated jobs as predicted, but the evolving economy created more than enough replacement jobs. Non-farm payroll jobs totaled 5.6 million statewide in December 1964 and, by December 1969, had jumped to over seven million. Over the next decade, the state economy continued its job expansion, reaching more than seventeen million payroll jobs in spring 2019.

The fact that automation and technology in the post-World War II period have resulted in net job gains does not mean this will be the outcome going forward. Researchers at MIT and elsewhere have begun to openly worry that the next phase of automation will be different, due to the role of artificial intelligence (AI).[8] AI is said to be eliminating jobs at a speed and scope well beyond past technological changes.

Whether the future calculus of job losses/gains due to AI will be different than the past remains to be determined. However, even if it is different, the nation will have the choice of how to respond. And in this response, for adults with autism and other developmental differences, it is jobs, rather than benefits or UBI, which should be the priority. As we shall see throughout the next pages, jobs play more important social and psychological roles for these adults than for most other adults. The pandemic has underscored these roles.

Eric Zigman is the director of the Golden Gate Regional Center, which serves more than 9,400 persons with developmental differences. Reflecting how most of these persons have been unemployed during the pandemic, he observes, "Most of our adults who were working prior to the pandemic have been furloughed or laid off. They intensely miss somewhere to go every day, with co-workers. They find a good deal of self-esteem in their jobs, no matter what the level or pay. Going forward, jobs, rather than guaranteed income, is what our participants seek."[9]

NOTES

1. There is lengthy academic literature, drawing on survey data, on the importance of employment for adults with developmental disabilities, including D. Nord et al, "The State of the Science of Employment and Economic Self-Sufficiency for People with Intellectual and Developmental Disabilities," *Intellectual and Developmental Disabilities*, 51(5), 376–384 (2013) and A. Milgore et al, "Integrated employment or sheltered workshops: Preferences of adults with intellectual disabilities, their families and staff," *Journal of Vocational Rehabilitation*, 265–19 (2007).

2. Michael Bernick, "Increasing Autism Employment: An Anthropologist's Perspective," *Forbes*, May 9, 2017.

3. G.J. Santoni, "The Employment Act of 1946: Some History Notes," Federal Reserve Bank of St. Louis, November 1986. https://files.stlouisfed.org/files /htdocs/publications/review/86/11/Employment_Nov1986.pdf.

4. Anne Roux, Paul Shattuck, "National Autism Indicators Report: 2017," A.J. Drexel Autism Institute, Drexel University, Philadelphia, 2017, https://drexel.edu/autismoutcomes/publications-and-reports/publications /National-Autism-Indicators-Report-Developmental-Disability-Services -and-Outcomes-in-Adulthood/.

5. "Employers and Recruiters", Autism Speaks, accessed January 23, 2021, https://www.autismspeaks.org/employers-recruiters.

6. The 85% unemployed/underemployed number is also cited for college graduates with autism in Nicole Lyn Pesce, "Most College Grads with Autism Can't Find Jobs," *Marketwatch*, April 2, 2019. https://www .marketwatch.com/story/most-college-grads-with-autism-cant-find-jobs -this-group-is-fixing-that-2017-04-10-5881421

7. Officials with the Cannery and Food Processing Workers detailed the rapid movement in processing from the mechanization that started in World War II to the advanced automation that the industry was currently undergoing. Food processing output was increasing in 1964, even as the number of workers declined. Similarly, the State Council of Carpenters detailed the new capital processes and newly established computer scheduling, cutting the need for construction workers on major infrastructure projects. Testimony of job loss even came from the Milk Wagon Drivers, Local 302, whose membership had dwindled to 1400 by 1964, due to the technological advances in maintaining perishable products. Union officials and others warned that California was facing a permanent decline in jobs.

8. Daron Acemoglu and Pascual Restrepo, "Robots and Jobs: Evidence from US Labor Markets", NBER Working Paper No 23285, March 2017, https://www.nber.org/papers/w23285; Eduardo Porter, "Jobs Threatened by Machines: A Once 'Stupid' Concern Gains Respect," *New York Times*, June 7, 2016.
9. Phone interview of Eric Zigman with author, October 5, 2020.

3

AUTISM EMPLOYMENT INITIATIVES AMONG PRIVATE SECTOR EMPLOYERS: LARGE AND SMALL

Autism employment initiatives in businesses have increased in the past decade. Expansion will draw on advocacy within their companies by adults with autism and family members, an overdue participation by universities and large non-profits, testing new forms of retention incentives, and, perhaps most of all, increasing the proven roles of the autism consultancies. These consultancies will engage midsize and small businesses, which up to now have been largely non-engaged.

Five years ago, a handful of major companies in the United States had autism employment initiatives. Today, there are over a hundred (including the more than twenty with the Autism at Work initiative), and prior to the pandemic more were being added each month, with Salesforce and VMWare among the newest additions. Further, a new subindustry of autism workforce consultancies has emerged: consultancies that are reaching out to employers to encourage intentional autism efforts, and assist in structuring these efforts.

The experiences of these initiatives and the autism workforce consultancies point to several actions for expanding targeted autism employment among large employers in the next few years. They are a mix of governmental and extra-governmental actions.

Over the past five years, few autism employment efforts have been undertaken with midsize and smaller firms. Expanding autism employment in these firms will also be a mix of actions, with a main role for the autism workforce consultancies that can aggregate expertise, tasks, and costs among firms.

Parts I and II summarize the current state of the autism initiatives in the private sector—by major companies and workforce consultancies—and the model they have identified for effective autism hiring and retention in private firms. Part III sets out paths for expansion.

Part I: The Targeted Autism Initiatives among America's Major Employers

Autism programs with large private sector employers have been the focus activity and research over the past decade. These programs have led to jobs for adults with autism. They have developed an effective model of recruitment, onboarding, retention, and support.

In her new book, *Employment and Disability*, Professor Susanne Bruyere of Cornell traces the history of these programs, and the model they have developed.[1] To summarize, a first wave of autism employment initiatives occurred in the early 2000s, which included two of America's largest retailers, Walgreens and Best Buy, as well as the mortgage giant Federal Home Loan Mortgage Company (Freddie Mac) and the financial services firm TIAA-CREF. In 2007, Walgreens launched a targeted retention effort for adults with autism as warehouse workers at a distribution center in Anderson, South Carolina, and subsequently expanded the initiative to other distribution centers. James Emmet, a rehabilitation counselor by trade, helped Walgreens set up these hiring programs and went on to create a similar autism employment program for Best Buy, at its distribution center near Louisville, Kentucky.

It was the autism employment initiative by software giant SAP, though, that launched the second and current wave of initiatives by major employers, notably by some of America's tech giants. The SAP "Autism at Work" program started in 2013, focused on hiring adults with autism in software testing and software engineering jobs. The program, which has gotten a good deal of media attention in the years since, set out a general template that included targeted hiring, job coaching, and an ongoing support network with the company.

The SAP program began with a few hires in the first cohort, but grew steadily to roughly 180 hires worldwide (roughly half in the United States) by 2019. It helped spur similar Autism at Work programs at Microsoft, DXC Technologies (formerly Hewlett Packard), JPMorgan Chase, EY, and Deloitte, as well as the establishment of an Autism at Work Employer Roundtable, and a well-attended annual Autism at Work conference.

In the past few years, SAP's targeted autism hiring has leveled off, but the other companies have steadily expanded their programs. On the eve of the pandemic in February 2020, JPMorgan Chase was nearing 180 hires, and EY and Microsoft each had around a hundred hires. Microsoft has come to assume leadership of the Autism at Work Roundtable in the past two years and used its influence to spur other corporate autism efforts.

The Microsoft program illustrates the structured hiring and retention mechanisms common to the programs. Like a good number of the autism initiatives, the Microsoft program was driven by parents within the company. In early 2015, two senior Microsoft officials, Corporate Vice President Mary Ellen Smith and Chief Accessibility Officer Jenny Lay-Flurrie, read of the SAP effort and tasked Neil Barnett, a graduate of Georgia Tech and member of the Accessibility department to follow up. Barnett researched the SAP program, and sought out adults with autism and practitioners for their employment perspectives. Microsoft launched its first cycle of five trainees in software engineering positions in May 2015. It subsequently has conducted regular training cycles, including through the pandemic.

The Microsoft training cycles since 2015 have each centered on five to ten open positions at the company, targeted for adults with autism. These positions have been mainly in software engineering, but more recently extended to jobs in marketing and administration. "Microsoft is a technology company, so the great majority of our Autism at Work participants are in technology jobs. Of the 100 or so placements so far, roughly 90% are in technology jobs," Barnett explains. "But we're expanding to other occupations for adults with autism without technology skills. We had planned a major push for Autism at Work in our retail stores, but this was halted when Microsoft decided this year to discontinue the retail stores."[2]

The Microsoft targeted hiring process starts with an application portal set aside for adults with autism. "Microsoft has always hired adults with autism; our current program, however, is an intentional program to boost both recruitment and retention," Barnett notes. Resumes submitted through the autism portal are reviewed in line with the identified positions at Microsoft, followed by pre-assessment interviews, and promising candidates are then invited to a four-day skills assessment at the Microsoft campus in Redmond with the hiring teams. "We learned that our traditional hiring process, the front door of Microsoft, could be a major barrier; by adjusting the shape of the door, we could help candidates showcase and demonstrate their talent to hiring managers."[3]

Following hiring, each Autism at Work participant is offered a job coach from Provail, a nonprofit in Seattle, specializing in supporting workers with disabilities. The job coach is connected both to the participant and to the team manager. The manager and other team members are offered training sessions on autism and other developmental differences.

Augmenting the job coach and team manager training, Microsoft assigns each participant a mentor from the company workforce, often an employee who has a child with autism and volunteers to be a mentor, along with access to the Employee Research Group for Microsoft employees with developmental differences. These elements are meant to foster retention and set an "autism friendly" work environment.

Not all of the other Autism at Work companies have the same level of program resources in hiring and retention as Microsoft. But these other companies all do have the three elements of targeted hiring, job coaching, and support structures, including training of supervisors and a number of support networks. Salesforce and VMWare are two other prominent tech companies that launched autism employment initiatives in 2019 and 2020, and both incorporate program staff and hiring/retention protocols.

While most of the Autism at Work programs are in tech or have targeted tech jobs, the Roundtable does include major employers with non-tech jobs. Cintas, the worldwide company in branded uniform and facility services with forty-five thousand employees, is one. For the past few years it has had autism (and disability) hiring initiatives focused on warehouse positions, and in fewer numbers in IT and Human Resources positions. Manufacturing giant Proctor and Gamble started an autism hiring initiative in 2019 (also driven by a family member working at the company).

Expanding initiatives outside of tech (and outside of urban centers) has become a priority of autism employment groups, including the national autism group, Autism Speaks. In 2019–2020, Autism Speaks has helped get two initiatives off the ground in the manufacturing field: with Stanley Black & Decker (SB&D), the tool company based in New Britain, Connecticut, and with Lee Container, a plastic fabrication company in Centerville, Iowa. The former, announced in Fall 2019, is a five-year initiative targeting jobs in the company's production facilities, and highlighting careers for adults with autism in manufacturing. SB&D's chief human resources officer tied the initiative to the aging of the manufacturing workforce: "New innovations could leave manufacturing with a gap of 3.5 million unfilled jobs in the next ten years."[4]

Part II: The New Subindustry of Autism Workforce Consultancies
The Autism at Work programs have received a good deal of the media attention, but represent only a segment of autism initiatives in private firms. Other private sector programs have been launched with the assistance of a new subindustry of autism workforce consultancies.

Integrate (formerly the Asperger Syndrome Training & Employment Partnership) was among the first of the autism workforce consultancies when former bank and insurance official Marcia Scheiner started it in New York in 2010. In the years since, Scheiner has been joined by more than twenty other autism workforce consultancies of some size: among them, Next for Autism, Neurodiversity Pathways, Evolibri, Uptimize, and Meristem—along with two of the other early consultancies, Autism Speaks and Specialisterne.

Together, these consultancies are now operating in a range of industry sectors and geographies. Though most are still connected to one or more of the tech or tech-related initiatives, they increasingly reach outside of tech.

Integrate is now a North American operation, with offices in Canada, as well as Ohio and California. It contracts with employers, and its revenues come primarily from its consulting services. It utilizes a structured process based on the four pillars it has identified with autism employment success: *Assessment, Education & Training, Recruitment,* and *Employment Support.* Scheiner briefly describes these pillars, and how they are implemented:

> Firms usually come to us because they have one or more people in the firm who have heard about and are interested in a targeted autism initiative. Often it is someone who has a family member, friend or neighbor with autism. In some cases, the impetus comes from someone in human resources or diversity

who has heard about neurodiversity, but that is rarer. We also do a lot of outreach to companies, and as well get referrals from some of the Autism at Work companies with current programs.[5]

Assessment: Integrate starts with asking the company officials, "What are your hiring needs?" Scheiner explains, "We want to know what positions they have difficulty filling and focus on those positions. We've learned that an autism hiring initiative works best if it is rooted in the hiring needs of the employer." The employer is encouraged to think about which departments might be good fits in terms of the managers and culture. "In choosing departments, we say to human resources staff we want 'volunteers' not 'voluntolds.'"

Education: Training on autism is offered to as wide a group in the firm as is interested—not only the line managers and other employees in the participating department, but other workers, especially senior management. Nobody is required to take the training, but Scheiner notes that so many people today have a connection to the autism world that attendance usually is substantial. Training covers what is autism, the range of skills and behaviors, the success of previous autism initiatives, and the problems that these programs have encountered.

Recruiting: Integrate connects with local autism groups and disability agencies to assist in recruitment. Integrate also advises companies on the screening process, especially how their interview process can be structured so as not to screen out good candidates.

Employment Support: Integrate holds weekly check-ins with the department managers. The check-ins may continue for three months or they may continue for a year or more, depending on the progress of the participant and issues raised by managers.[6]

"We advise our firms to start with pilot projects, and most start with four to ten slots, so that the numbers are not large. But we think that the best way to grow is to build on successes," Scheiner said.

Other consultancies draw on variants of these elements of assessment, training, recruitment, and retention. Next for Autism is the largest of the consultancies, with a client base that includes Staples, Cintas, and Quest Diagnostics. Next for Autism describes its mission as partnering with corporations "to attract, hire and retain employees with autism and other disabilities." It offers a set of four services similar to the four pillars of Integrate: designing autism inclusion in collaboration with the corporate partner, training for C-suite managers and employees about autism and disability awareness, recruiting candidates, and providing on-going support to scale and sustain programs.

While Integrate and Next for Autism focus on employer partnerships, some of the other consultancies also are engaged in training and coaching, along with partnerships. Neurodiversity Pathways, based in San Jose in the heart of Silicon Valley, is one of the more recently formed consultancies. It was founded in January 2018 by Ranga Jayaraman. After obtaining his PhD in Engineering from Stanford University in 1982, Jayaraman held senior positions in information technology with IBM, Hitachi, and Stanford Business School for more than thirty-five years, before starting Neurodiversity Pathways.

Neurodiversity Pathways is both a job training/placement entity and consultancy. In its training, it operates a series of six-week employment boot camps for adults with autism (with sections on "personal effectiveness skills," job search skills, and workplace behavior skills), with four to eight adults per boot camp. The participants are usually clients of the state vocational rehabilitation department, which has assumed the costs of the training and accompanying job placement. Neurodiversity Pathways has enrolled nearly sixty participants in these boot camps.

With his background in information technology, Jayaraman in his first year focused on sourcing candidates to the Autism at Work and related tech initiatives, but today is focused outside of tech. "I came to see these initiatives, mainly requiring tech skills, were fits for only a small segment of the adults with autism that were coming to us."[7] Neurodiversity Pathways recently started its first partnership outside of tech with a major electrical contractor in the South Bay.

In its employer partnerships, Neurodiversity Pathways has grappled with behaviors of its participants that undermine employment: "So many of the adults with autism coming to us have comorbidities— behaviors that get in the way of easy integration into workplaces, whether these behaviors relate to time management, talking to themselves, obsessive compulsive behaviors, or tens of others. We need to push adults to adapt. But my hope is that we can get more employers to meet us halfway."

Jayaraman has come to market an "Employment First" model to employers. He urges employers to utilize the current subsidies for adults who are clients of the developmental disabilities department. He urges employers and the department to think of a placement for up to six months, adding, "I tell them our participants can take some time to train and integrate into the workforce and they need to be given time rather than being fired for the first mistake or inappropriate behavior."

Nearby Neurodiversity Pathways in Santa Clara is Evo Libri, a job coaching and autism consultancy headed by Jan Johnston Tyler since 2007. Like Jayaraman, Johnston Tyler also came to autism employment with a background in the tech field (DHS Systems, Juniper Networks, and Cisco Systems). Evo Libri started with a job coaching practice, and was one of the first job coaching firms in California specializing in adults with autism. Evo Libri continues its coaching practice, both with private pay clients (engineers at Apple, Google, and Facebook who seek advice in navigating the workplace), and referrals from vocational rehabilitation.[8] In the past few years, Johnston

Tyler has expanded her efforts, consulting with businesses interested in implementing structured autism initiatives.

Prior to the pandemic, Johnston Tyler was part of the targeted autism initiatives developed at Salesforce and VMWare, and part of the job coaching structure with a number of the Autism at Work projects. She notes that most autism initiatives still are aimed at a small segment of the adult autism community with tech skills, perhaps 10–15 percent by her estimate. Human resources and diversity departments are only beginning to think about neurodiversity, if they are at all, and move very slowly. Most of all she notes that "While all of us agree that targeted autism initiatives are a good idea, none of us has really cracked the code on how to scale these initiatives within firms or across firms."[9]

Part III: Expanding Autism Employment Initiatives among Private Employers

What will it take to "crack the code" in Johnston Tyler's words and expand autism hiring and initiatives in private firms? Here are some of the main paths suggested from the autism employment efforts and other targeted employment efforts of the past decade.

Achieving and Documenting Hiring and Retention Results

The foundation for any expansion lies with the employers currently engaged in targeted autism employment, and their ability to achieve and document results, and reach out to colleagues.

Microsoft's Barnett sees the process of expanding the corporate initiatives as a gradual one, with more employers becoming involved as the current programs show results. He notes that the Autism at Work Roundtable was gaining momentum prior to the pandemic, and expects this to restart when the pandemic ends: "The first months of 2020, we were getting three to four calls a week from companies around the nation who were interested in starting autism at work efforts. When the pandemic came, the calls stopped; but we expect to restart when the pandemic ends and the economy more fully reopens. We need to successfully place and retain participants."[10]

A similar view is put forward by Brian Jacobs, a veteran venture capitalist who invests in companies employing adults with autism. Jacobs sees the process of expanding these corporate initiatives as tied to results, noting, "The best marketing will be as more and more of the Autism at Work and other initiatives show results. This will happen; it will just take some time."[11]

Indeed, the most effective scaling for employment programs outside of autism over the past four decades has been to show results, in hiring and retention. This has been true for scaling the hiring/retention strategies for other groups whose high unemployment has been of concern to policymakers: the long-term employed, ex-offenders, and welfare recipients.

The scaling of America Works, and its approach for placing welfare recipients, illustrates scaling through results. Peter Cove and his wife and colleague, Lee Bowes, started America Works in 1984, with a model of "work first," then a contrarian view in the employment field. The idea at the center of this model: welfare recipients benefit most not from lengthy education, training, or counseling programs, but rather from direct placement into a job. Once people are placed in jobs, they often find ways on their own to address other "static" or challenges in their lives. Cove explained in his 2019 book, *Poor No More: Rethinking Dependency and the War on Poverty*: "When some mothers on welfare came to us, they often explained that they could not work because they had no day care. We would still send them on a job interview, and when the company wanted to hire them, miraculously, they found a grandmother or daycare center."[12]

Cove and Bowes invested their own funds to get America Works off the ground. As America Works demonstrated results, it slowly began to win contracts with local and state governments.

America Works' "work first" model was by no means universally embraced. Welfare rights advocates heatedly denounced America

Works, claiming that it pushed welfare recipients into "modern slavery" of lower wage jobs. Cove regularly pushed back that middle class is the goal, but service providers needed to start with the jobs that were realistic. America Works was able to survive and expand, not because of political influence, but because it was able to demonstrate placements. It opened its processes and data to researchers outside of America Works (including researchers hostile to America Works), to confirm placements and retention. It encouraged employers who were thinking of taking on America Works participants to speak with employers who had done so.

By 2019, America Works had grown to twenty-eight cities. It is now one of the largest job placement entities in America for welfare recipients, ex-offenders, and workers with developmental differences.

Several elements of America Works' story are relevant to autism employment. Autism practitioners will contribute to expansion as they proceed with the same documentation and transparency as America Works, emphasize retention as well as placement, and encourage their employers to reach out to colleagues.

The Heightened Role of Family Members in Promoting Hiring Initiatives in Their Own Firms

Autism employment initiatives in major businesses will grow through a heightened role of parents and family members in promoting hiring initiatives in their own firms. Family members have played a key role in launching the autism hiring initiatives that currently exist: SAP, Microsoft, JPMorgan Chase, VMWare, and Proctor and Gamble, to name a few.

Professor Susanne Bruyere identifies "messaging from top leadership" as a main factor in whether an autism employment initiative is actually implemented, and has any staying power. She writes of the senior leadership roles in the Autism at Work programs, driven by family members:

Sending the message that affirmative hiring of autistic individuals is a part of the company's strategic direction affirms that employees need to take this initiative seriously and treat it as a business imperative rather than a 'corporate social responsibility' or community engagement opportunity.[13]

Bruyere adds, "Company representatives that reported having strong senior management commitment to diversity were five times more likely to have hired a person with a disability in the past year."[14]

Most adults with autism and family members are not in senior positions. To be sure, their ability to influence company hiring will be less. Yet, many large companies now have "Employee Resource Groups" that can provide an avenue for advocacy. Employees at all job levels can serve as mentors to adults with autism. This mentorship is part of both the SAP and Microsoft initiatives.

An Overdue Role for Universities, Private Foundations, and Large Non-profits

Universities, private foundations, and large non-profits all have been notably absent as participants in autism employment initiatives. This is so even though these entities in most cases have greater flexibility, more relaxed work environments, and greater alignment of autism employment with their social service and public welfare missions.

Jayaraman and Johnston Tyler have both sought to reach out to Bay Area universities with no success. Jayaraman explains, "I make the same pitch to universities as I do to other employers: our adults with autism are gold, if you give them a chance they will bring loyalty and a positive approach to your worksite. But the universities are proving to be even more difficult to engage than the large companies."[15]

The failure to participate in autism hiring extends even to the university-based autism research centers that are receiving millions from federal and state governments. The University of California, San Francisco (UCSF) Medical Center, is one of these centers, with various autism research projects including a Center for Autism Spectrum Disorders. Several hiring requests have been made to UCSF by Bay Area practitioners seeking placements, and UCSF has demurred. UCSF has declined to participate in hiring, even when the wages of proposed autism internships have been fully subsidized. In one case, a UCSF research project declined to take on an intern, when it learned that it could not obtain a few additional dollars to pay for administration and supervision.

University-based autism research centers should be taking the lead not only in hiring adults with autism, but also in encouraging other parts of the university to do so. They should be taking the lead in addressing the inertia and bureaucracy that exist in universities and undermine autism hiring initiatives.

The Act will recognize the role of universities as employers for adults with autism. More strongly, it might begin to tie any federal or state autism research expenditures to hiring goals.

Similarly, major non-profits and private foundations should be leaders in autism hiring, given their social orientations. They should not need to be pushed or required to do so. The Act, though, will encourage and recognize their role, and nexus to their missions. For major non-profits, it might also tie funding they receive for social services, job training, or mental health projects to hiring within these nonprofits.

Universities, non-profits, and foundations are important in autism hiring given the size of their workforces. Further, these entities are not under the same economic pressures as private employers and should be able to more fully exercise the patience and flexibility for effective autism hiring and retention.

Investing in the Autism Workforce Consultancies to Aggregate Expertise, Costs, and Tasks among Midsize and Small Firms

Currently, most states offer one or more of the following four sets of financial incentives to spur hiring and retention of adults with disabilities:

(i) Direct wage subsidies through state funds for hiring workers with disabilities: Many states subsidize hiring and retention of workers with disabilities out of state budgets. The subsidies range in amount and time period. California's Paid Internship Program is one of the more generous. It subsidizes the wages of workers who are enrolled with the state department of developmental services, at minimum wage or higher, for 100 percent of wages up to $10,400 per year. The subsidy stops once the $10,400 amount is reached in a year's period, but can be renewed for additional years. For employers, there is the additional advantage that the worker is hired by a third party intermediary, who takes care of all of the onboarding and payroll functions.

(ii) On the job training and work experience funds under the federal Workforce Innovation and Opportunity Act (WIOA): The federal workforce funds under WIOA, administered by state and local workforce boards, contain funds which can be used to incentivize hiring of workers with a range of disabilities. Workers with disabilities are eligible for Work Experience, which can be up to 100 percent of wages for several months, and for on-the-job training, which can be up to 50 percent or even 75 percent of wages—for weeks or up to three to four months.

(iii) The Work Opportunity Tax Credit: Employers who hire workers with disabilities can receive a federal tax credit of $1200-$9600 depending on the length of employment and wages earned.

(iv) Job coaches: When deemed needed to help a worker learn the skills and behaviors needed for the job, state disability departments and vocational rehabilitation departments provide job coaches at no cost to the employers. The job coaching is sometimes done on-site, sometimes remotely. It is expected to be gradually reduced over time.

With large businesses, these financial incentives have not significantly impacted hiring decisions. Among these businesses, the hiring tax credit is sometimes utilized, but has not been a motivator in hiring. Nor have the other wage subsidies. The offer of the job coach is sometimes taken up, but usually because the company does not have the expertise in house.

Few midsize and small businesses have made use of these incentives. These firms have been largely absent from the structured autism employment programs. They generally have no idea that wage subsidies or job coaches are even available.

The drafters of the Act will want to consider how the current financial incentives might be revised, particularly to better incentivize retention. Any future incentives should be aimed at not only hiring, but setting structures and a workplace ethos in place to keep employees on board.

Beyond incentives, the Act will look to the workforce consultancies to grow their partnerships with large firms, and even more so to engage midsize and small firms. It is the midsize and small firms—firms with fewer than a hundred workers that currently employ around 33.4 percent of all private sector workers—that constitute an untapped autism market.[16]

Consider the current obstacles for midsize and small firms. These firms do not have the expertise or resources to administer the type of structured hiring and retention program that autism employment initiatives have found to be best practices. These firms rarely have the resources to handle the paperwork and reimbursement delays associated with most government hiring subsidies. Additionally, these firms have less bandwidth than large employers to address performance issues that arise.

Consider how a broadened system of workforce consultancies, abetted by the Act, might address these obstacles. In such a system, individual consultancies would partner with multiple midsize and small businesses to provide the expertise and resources to these firms for assessment and recruitment. The consultancies would help address performance issues and structures for retention. They would identify potential hiring credits, subsidies or job coaches, and handle the associated paperwork.

Further, the consultancies might assume additional roles to make the hiring and retention process easier for businesses. A consultancy could serve as the employer-of-record: freeing the small or midsize business from the responsibilities for payrolling and ensuring compliance with worker taxes and regulations. Since it operates among numerous firms, it could transfer a worker who may not be a good fit in one firm to try another firm, rather than giving up on the worker.

What would it mean for the Act to invest in this consultancy system? To test such a system, the Act could provide funding targeted at serving midsize and small businesses. Funding initially would be for a few years to give the consultancies time to prove their value. The funding would need to be carefully designed, to be linked to job placements. It would not go to social welfare groups that provide no placements. The autism consultancies that have arisen so far, though, have a strong sense of mission, and most of the founders are volunteering a good deal of their time. Safeguards are needed, but it is likely that even with public funding, this sense of mission will prevail.

***

AUTISM EMPLOYMENT PRACTITIONERS at the Autism at Work companies and with the consultancies might well read the strategies for expansion noted above, and say, "But you've missed the main selling point for expansion: the talent advantage that adults with autism can bring to a company!"

Indeed, talent advantage is a main theme of the consultancies and autism advocates today. As we look more closely into this talent advantage, though, we find it more complex than often presented by advocates and very different across the autism spectrum.

NOTES

1. Susanne Bruyere, *Employment and Disability: Issues, Innovations and Opportunities*, Labor and Employment Relations Association, University of Illinois, Champaign, Illinois, 2019.
2. Neil Barnett, Talk to the AASCEND Job Club, August 1, 2020.
3. Neil Barnett, Talk to the AASCEND Job Club, August 1, 2020.
4. "NxtGen Program Develops an Inclusive Workplace for Adults with Autism", accessed January 23, 2021, https://www.stanleyblackanddecker .com/article/nxtgen-program-develops-inclusive-workplace-adults-autism
5. Marcia Scheiner, Talk to the AASCEND Job Club, October 10, 2020.
6. Regarding Employment Support, Scheiner adds: "We have specialized in a segment of the autism community: those who have a college degree or at least some college. They have their own difficulties in finding and holding jobs. What this means, though, is that we do not have the more intensive employment supports, such as the onsite job coaches, built into some of the other programs."
7. Ranga Jayaraman, phone interview with author, September 2, 2020.
8. In an earlier book, *The Autism Job Club*, I wrote about Johnston Tyler's art as an autism job coach.
9. Jan Johnston Tyler, phone interview with author, September 4, 2020.
10. Neil Barnett, Talk to the AASCEND Job Club, August 1, 2020.
11. Brian Jacobs, phone interview with author, July 25, 2020.
12. Peter Cove, *Poor No More: Rethinking Dependency and the War on Poverty*, New Brunswick, New Jersey, Transation Publishers, 2017, 2.
13. Susanne Bruyere, *Employment and Disability: Issues, Innovations and Opportunities*, Labor and Employment Relations Association, University of Illinois, Champaign, Illinois, 2019, 267.
14. Ibid.
15. Ranga Jayaraman, phone interview with author, September 2, 2020.
16. Firms with fewer than twenty workers employ 16.8 percent of the private sector workforce. Small Business & Entrepreneurship Council, "Facts and Data on Small Business and Entrepreneurship," retrieved September 2020, https://sbecouncil.org/about-us/facts-and-data/.

4

AUTISM "TALENT ADVANTAGE"

Marketing adults with autism as a talent pipeline is an effective approach. But the talent advantage will in nearly all cases not be the tech and savant skills that are prominent in the media. It will be found elsewhere.

"Our autism employment program markets the autism talent advantage" explains Luther Jackson, a manager at the NOVA Workforce Board in Silicon Valley overseeing autism initiatives. "The emphasis is not on social responsibility, but on the skills that adults with autism bring to the workplace."[1] Adults with autism as an overlooked talent pipeline is a theme now widely adopted by Workforce Boards, like NOVA, as well as the autism workforce intermediaries and the Autism at Work employers.

Marketing adults with autism as a talent pipeline is an effective approach today: it is consistent with the embrace of the talent pipeline concept more generally among human resources staff and industry associations, and it highlights productivity. However, as noted in the previous chapter, the tech talents most often called out in this approach are present in only a small segment of the adult autism population. The wider talent pipeline of the adult autism community encompasses other skills, and especially other personal attributes. Identifying the specific talent skills and attributes in each individual will be key to marketing success.

Part I: Recent Autism at Work and Related Programs are Finding a Segment of the Adult Autism Community Can Function Well in Certain Tech Jobs, But This Is a Small Segment

DXC Technology in Australia (formerly Hewlett Packard Enterprise) has operated one of the leading Autism at Work initiatives since 2014. Called the Dandelion Program, it has employed 120 adults with autism and other neurodiverse conditions in eleven DXC Dandelion teams across Australia, through the end of 2019.[2] These adults are placed in three main fields: software testing, data analytics, and cybersecurity. They work in "pods": teams of eight to nine adults with autism employed collaboratively with the large government entities, financial institutions, and major corporations that are DXC's client base.

The Dandelion program has been successful on several measures. It has been sustained over six years, and grown from one government department, the Human Services department, to the current eleven sites. It has collaborated with Cornell's Institute on Employment and Disability to develop and source a curriculum on hiring and retention. It has developed "Neurodiversity Hubs" to connect adults with autism at universities with post-university employment.

Further, it has sought to document and quantify the benefits of hiring adults with autism. In its first years, it agreed to be a case study for Harvard Business School professor Gary Pisano and Robert Austin.[3] The researchers, drawing on data provided by DXC, reported that the pods of autism workers were 30 percent more productive than pods of other workers undertaking similar tasks.

Michael Fieldhouse, the Dandelion program architect, also has enlisted researchers at LaTrobe University to carefully observe and document the greater employee productivity. Fieldhouse has spoken frequently of the DXC autism pods as achieving a higher level quality of testing than other software testing pods, demonstrating greater thoroughness and focus.

Other Autism at Work employers also are trumpeting an "autism advantage" in software testing, coding, and data analytics. In an article entitled, "JP Morgan Found Autistic People Have Special Coding Powers," a JPMC program manager, Anthony Pacilio, declared that the autism hires as coders have outperformed other candidates. He cited one autism candidate who learned Java coding within a weekend, adding, "This speaks to the focus and dedication of people on the spectrum, part of his autism was his ability to learn things quickly."[4] James Mahoney, chief quality officer for the Mortgage Banking Technology division at JPMC, who has headed the Autism at Work effort, told a recent JPMC event on disability hiring that after three to six months working in his division, the workers with autism are "doing the work of people who took three years to ramp up, and were even 50 percent more productive."[5]

EY (Ernst and Young, LLP), an Autism at Work company, set up Centers of Excellence (CoE) at offices around the country, starting in Philadelphia in 2016 and Dallas in 2017, to employ adults with autism in tech positions related to its cybersecurity, robotics, and process automation businesses. A recent EY internal report was glowing in its praise of the CoE as demonstrating the mathematical, pattern recognition, and information processing skills of adults with autism. It is worth highlighting as it reflects the corporate communications connected with corporate autism initiatives:

> Neurodiverse individuals are often technologically inclined and detail-oriented, with strong skills in analytics, mathematics, pattern recognition and information processing— among the very skills businesses most urgently need. They thrive on predictability and can be especially tenacious and loyal workers who prefer to stay with one organization rather than move from opportunity to opportunities.

Companies are finding that people with autism approach problems differently, and that their logical straightforward thinking can spur process improvements that greatly increase productivity.[6]

What to make of this?

The experiences at EY and the other companies show that some individuals diagnosed with autism are able to bring strong tech skills. EY, SAP, Microsoft, and other companies have found a talent advantage, and their programs should grow.

But employment professionals and practitioners agree that these skills are present in a small segment of the adult autism community. As noted in the previous chapter, autism practitioners Jayaraman and Johnston Tyler estimate it to be 10–15 percent of the autism population.

When the idea that adults with autism possessed hidden tech skills was first popularized in the 2013–2014 period, with the announcement of the SAP program, many parents thought of it as the "Employment Answer." I did for a time for my son William, who was a student then at Cal State University East Bay, and trying to find a career fit. But it soon became apparent that William had no special tech skills, just as it soon became apparent to other parents that their daughters and sons did not have special tech skills.

At AASCEND, we've had three of our members hired in the Autism at Work program at SAP. Two of them are still at SAP and one has left. All three were having difficulty finding a steady job prior to SAP, and the program was a boon to them. But they had mathematical and computational skills that the majority of our AASCEND members do not.

Additionally, it's worth noting that all of the Autism at Work programs involve a competitive hiring process, drawing on applicants from throughout the nation. Only a small segment have the tech skills to be competitive.

Part II: Other Skills and Attributes Common across the Autism Community that Practitioners are Marketing as Forms of Talent Advantage

But if tech skills form a limited talent pipeline, other skills and attributes of talent are more widely distributed among adults with autism. These are the skills and attributes that autism employment practitioners are now focusing on.

Marcia Scheiner and colleagues at the consultancy Integrate have prepared a presentation to companies on "Why should your company hire professionals with autism?"

Scheiner answers: "There is a very compelling reason why companies should be interested in understanding autism and successfully employing individuals on the spectrum: *It's good for business.*" She sets out six business reasons, including three related to talent advantage: (i) reduced staff turnover, (ii) increased productivity, and (iii) competitive advantage.[7]

In discussing reduced staff turnover, Scheiner writes that from her past decade of work in the field, she has found that adults with autism are loyal employees. They "tend to dislike change and will stay in the same job for a long time if the work and the work environment are appropriate." She singles out certain skills related to productivity and competitive advantage, including "focus, attention to detail, accuracy, memory of facts and figures, and ability to concentrate on repetitive tasks and procedures."[8]

Other autism employment consultancies are making similar talent arguments: a talent pipeline not of tech skills, but of focus, attention to detail, concentration, loyalty, and appreciation for the job. The Meristem autism consultancy has produced a "Transformative Autism Program" Manual for California Employers that starts, "While people on the spectrum exhibit a wide range of abilities and personalities, in general they share traits and tendencies that are positive for most workplaces." Meristem singles out: attention to detail, ability to detect patterns and retain large amounts of information, and affinity for repetitive tasks.[9]

This talent identification is not meant to apply to every adult with autism. Most adults with autism in fact will not have all of the skills noted, and a good number will have none of these skills. The academic research on skills associated with autism is still in initial stages. But the limited research that does exist suggests that these skills are more widespread among adults with autism than in the general population, and worth trying to apply to the employment question.[10]

In his advancing of autism employment, Dr. Lawrence Fung of Stanford has compiled a "Strengths Based Model of Neurodiversity." Too often it is the deficiencies of adults with autism that are focused on, which can lead to negativity and immobility on the part of these adults. Instead, the talent advantages should be the focus. Dr. Fung identifies these strengths as: persistence, detail oriented, fund of knowledge, concrete/honest, and loyal.[11] Through the Stanford Neurodiversity Project, Fung is reaching out to both employers and adults and developing registries of jobs and job seekers.

Part III: Identifying the Talent Advantage for Each Individual with Autism

Dr. Fung recently wrote about one of the adults with autism who is part of the Stanford Neurodiversity Project, Mark, who does not have the strengths of being especially detail oriented or able to detect patterns, or with strong memory. But Mark has been able to get and hold jobs based on the advocacy of his parents and on other strengths or talent advantages that employers recognized and valued: the loyalty that Fung singles out as a strength prevalent across the spectrum, as well as Mark's positive nature. Fung's description of Mark is worth quoting at some length:

> Mark will soon be forty years old and with the exception of only a few months has been employed for the last thirty years. He has had a full time job for the last twenty years—for nine years as a janitor for a Fitness Club and for the past eleven

years for Draeger's Market in the Blackhawk Plaza in Danville . . . When he graduated from high school, it was expected that he would receive SSI benefits. He tried this, but this led to such anxiety because when he did work it would take months for the government to adjust his benefits. Mark made the decision to stop SSI. Mark wanted to work full time—he does not see himself as disabled—he sees himself as very able. Mark has also made the decision he wants to work until he is 80. Being able to work gives Mark great joy and a purpose in life.[12]

Mark and his mother Lauren have been members of AASCEND for the past decade. Mark comes from time to time to our Autism Job Club, even though he is not looking for a job. The qualities of loyalty and a sunny disposition that Mark possesses should count for something in the job market. In my experience, most employers do not give appropriate consideration to these talent advantages of adults with autism (employers too often focus on the deficiencies). Mark is fortunate to have found an employer who does recognize this talent advantage.

The talent advantages for each adult with autism will differ. Nearly always, these advantages will be outside of tech, and often outside of measurable skills. They may be in the realm of job appreciation, enthusiasm, or stability. But that does not make these advantages less real. It is up to job counselors and coaches to identify and market these advantages.

NOTES

1. Luther Jackson, phone interview with author, August 31, 2020.
2. DXC Technology, "DXC Dandelion Program: 2019 in Review," https://www.dxc.technology/au/ds/142241/142242-about_the_dxc_dandelion_program (retrieved August 2020).

3. Gary Pisano and Robert Austin, "Hewlett Packard Enterprise: The Dandelion Program," *Harvard Business School Case Studies*, September 8, 2016.

4. Sarah Butcher, "JP Morgan Found Autistic People Have Special Coding Powers," efinancialcareers.com, June 15, 2020, retrieved September 2020, https://news.efinancialcareers.com/us-en/3003960/jpmorgan-found-autistic -people-have-special-coding-powers.

5. "Disability as an Asset in the Workplace," accessed September 2, 2020, https://www.jpmorganchase.com/corporate/news/stories/disability-as -an-asset-in-the-workplace.htm.

6. "Neurodivesity: Driving Innovation from Unexpected Places", EY, accessed January 23, 2021, file:///C:/Users/msbernick/Downloads/ey-neurodiversity -driving-innovation-from-unexpected-places.pdf, 8.

7. Marcia Scheiner, *An Employer's Guide to Managing Professionals on the Autism Spectrum*, London, Jessica Kingsley Publishers, 2017, 26–29.

8. Marcia Scheiner, Talk to AASCEND Job Club, October 10, 2020.

9. Meristem, "Transformative Autism Program: Training Manual for California Employers," Meristem, Sacramento, California, 2020, https: //tapautism.org/.

10. Roundtable, "An Expert Discussion on Strengths-Based Approaches in Autism," *Autism in Adulthood*, Volume 1, No, 2, 2019, https://www .liebertpub.com/doi/pdf/10.1089/aut.2019.29002.aju; Scott Kauffman, "Autism: More Than Meets the Eye," *Scientific American*, June 19, 2019, https://blogs.scientificamerican.com/beautiful-minds/autism-more-than -meets-the-eye/.

11. Lawrence Fung, "Strengths Based Model of Neurodiversity and the Stanford Neurodiversity Project," Stanford University, 2020, https://med.stanford .edu/neurodiversity/NaW.html.

12. Lawrence Fung, e-mail to Special Interest Group on Neurodiversity of the Stanford Neurodiversity Project, September 4, 2020.

5

ARTHUR MILLER'S SON

The playwright Arthur Miller ("America's playwright") and his third wife Inge Morath in 1966 had a son Daniel with Down Syndrome, whom they placed in an institution soon after his birth and did not identify publicly for decades. The story only reached a wider audience in the past few years through a documentary by Miller's daughter Rebecca Miller. While the story carries several themes, a main one linked to autism employment is the talent advantage of Daniel Miller, how his father failed to recognize it, and how Daniel was able to find a place in the job market and an independent life.

Rebecca Miller's 2017 documentary was the first that most Americans learned of Daniel Miller and his institutionalization at the Southbury Training School in Connecticut in 1970, but not the first mention. In a deeply researched 2007 essay, "Arthur Miller's Missing Act," *Vanity Fair* writer Suzanna Andrews tracked Daniel's institutionalization, spoke to family and friends, and followed Daniel's life after leaving Southbury.[1]

As Andrews recounts, soon after Daniel was born in 1966, the doctors recognized the boy's condition and informed Miller. Within a short time, Miller decided that the boy could not be brought up in the Miller household and needed to be sent away. He was first sent to a home for infants in New York and then at age four to Southbury, an institution for persons with Down Syndrome and other developmental differences.

Andrews presents a grim picture of Southbury in the 1970s during Daniel's stay. When Southbury opened in 1940, it was meant as a model of enlightened treatment for the disabled, with handsome neo-Georgian brick buildings on 1600 acres in central Connecticut, and a school and job training programs. As Andrews describes, by the early 1970s when Daniel was placed there, it was understaffed and overcrowded, with nearly 2300 residents, living in rooms with thirty to forty beds. Southbury employees at the time recall no education or training, and residents warehoused in front of televisions.

According to Andrews, Miller declined to visit Daniel, but Morath did so on a regular basis. A friend recalls Morath commenting, "You know I go in there and it's like a Hieronymus Bosch painting."

Despite these conditions, several former Southbury workers describe Daniel as "a very friendly happy guy," well-liked by staff, always positive. Deborah Bowen, a disability rights advocate, recounts meeting Daniel in Southbury around 1980, and told Andrews, "He was just a delight, eager, happy, outgoing—in those days even more so than now, because of his isolation." Bowen recalls that Daniel showed her his room which he shared with twenty other people and his dresser with its few clothes. "I remember very clearly trying to respond with happiness, but it was very hard . . . His sole possession was this little tiny transistor radio with earplugs. It was something you'd pick up at a five-and-dime. And he was so proud to have it."

Andrews notes that at the end of his life Miller did acknowledge Daniel and include him in his will for a generous amount. But she is clearly critical of Miller's actions, quoting friends who speculate that Miller feared the disturbance to his work, or losing Morath's attention, or his shame at having a son who would embarrass him. "Miller excised a central character who didn't fit the plot of his life as he wanted it," she concludes.

In the early 1980s, Daniel was released from Southbury. He lived first in a group home with five housemates and later in an apartment with a roommate, through a supported living program. He obtained a bank account and a job at a supermarket. Most recently he has lived with an elderly couple, in a separate wing built for him.

Daniel Miller seems to have a far fuller life than envisioned for him in the 1960s. He continues at his job at the supermarket, even though he no longer needs the money. He has a circle of friends. He is active in disability advocacy groups.

The documentary does not give details of his activities (or his inner life). But Bowen, the disability activist, who still gets together with Daniel, tells Andrews, "He's made a life for himself; he is deeply valued and very, very loved. What a loss for Arthur Miller that he couldn't see how extraordinary his son is."

NOTE

1. Suzanna Andrews, "Arthur Miller's Missing Act" *Vanity Fair*, September 2007.

6

THE AUTISM JOB CLUBS AND MUTUAL SUPPORT

The Autism Job Clubs and other mutual support entities complement the governmental efforts. They do not need funding in the Act, though their roles and values need to be recognized in the Act.

Adults with autism and family members who find their way to our Autism Job Club in the Bay Area usually come bewildered by the job search process and with little idea of the resources available to them.

They may have read something about the Autism at Work programs at SAP or Microsoft, but soon recognize these jobs are few, they're located some distance from where they live, and are fits only for a small segment of adults with autism who have tech expertise. They may have applied for jobs through online process, and wonder why they're getting no responses. Family members want to help, but don't know where to start. They worry that their sons or daughters or siblings might never be employed.

Based on our Job Club experiences over the past decade, we tell them: "You will be employed, there is a place in the job market for you. But you need to take responsibility and actions on your own, and you need to join with others in the autism community in mutual support measures." And then we ask them to join us in the job placement process.

Part I: Our Autism Job Club Is Now in Its Ninth Year, and Our Members Range Across the Autism Spectrum in Skills and Interests

Our Autism Job Club of the Bay Area is now in its ninth year. On the first Saturday of each month, adults with autism, family members, and advocates continue to come to the Arc Building at 11th and Howard in downtown San Francisco, just as they have since November 2011.

Some of the original participants still come regularly, even though they have jobs. Andrew Bixler has been working at the Amazon Fulfillment Center on Potrero Hill for the past year. He comes each month, as does Jim Ullrey, our eldest member now at seventy-seven, who has been doing contract assembly work, and Mark, who's been working at a grocery store in Danville. They all like the social element and it gives them something to do on the weekend.

As from the Club's first days, everyone is welcome. Attendance is around thirty to forty participants each month, a mix of adults on the spectrum and family members. The Club has a core group at any time, but also continues to benefit from a constant influx of new participants. AASCEND now has a mailing list of over eight hundred people in the Bay Area, and each month usually brings at least four or five new faces.

For the first few years, the Club was centered on job search techniques, but as membership began to decline (there's only so many sessions that can be done on resume writing) we pivoted to the current structure, which features guest speakers from the region's major employers. Speakers from online game companies, including Niantic and Zynga, always get a good crowd (many of the participants want to work for these game companies). Salesforce, Amazon, Pinterest, and Airbnb also have been popular.

In addition to these talks are the talks by adults with autism about their employment, including recent ones by longtime AASCEND member, Ethan, a librarian at a local college, and a panel on self-employment by AASCEND board members Stacey (who has had her pet sitting business since 2011) and Paul (home services business). We have not abandoned the job search techniques, however. Following the speakers, Keith, an AASCEND member and professional recruiter, leads a job search session, on resume writing, interviewing, and networking.

The participants continue to represent a wide range of skills, educational backgrounds, and interests. A few, perhaps 10 percent, have advanced educational backgrounds and skills. Ian, thirty-three, one of the regulars, graduated from Dominican University and did graduate work in cognitive psychology at the University of California, Santa Cruz. On his resume he describes himself as a "skilled researcher and analyst with 5+ years of experience gathering and evaluating data, designing research and conducting experiments." He's had project work since 2013, but is still searching for the steady employment he seeks. Jennifer, thirty-six, has a Master's degree from Cal State University East Bay in statistics. She too has had irregular project work, including a one-year stint with Apple and another with Stanford University, and is seeking a steady job.

Around 50 percent of the participants have some post-secondary education. Medhi recently completed a two-year course at Meristem, a craft-based program in the Sacramento area for adults on the spectrum, and Clara is starting this same program in the Fall. Chris graduated from San Francisco State this past summer and came with his father Miguel. Jonathan is at California State University East Bay now.

Most of the remaining 40 percent do have a high school degree. Justin completed high school and is currently unemployed and taking Lindamood Bell courses in reading comprehension for adults with developmental differences. His father Todd had heard about the Club and came with Justin seeking work experience opportunities.

We recognize that a significant segment of the autism community is more severely impacted, who do not have high school degrees, who have limited language or no language. We do not yet have the resources to help place these adults. For now, we connect them to the more intensive employment services available through the Regional Center.

Part II: Job Search Self-help and Mutual Support

"Ben, What's the Answer? How did you do it?" Willy asks his brother Ben in *Death of a Salesman*. Ben went into the African jungle when he was seventeen and came out when he was twenty-one and through the diamond trade became a rich man. Willy is searching for direction on how his two grown sons, Biff and Happy, similarly can succeed financially and be important people in the economy.

Our adult members with autism are not especially seeking to get rich, or to be important people in the economy. They are searching usually for something more modest: a steady position, with benefits, some place to go every day and have a recognized job.

Our members with autism have gotten jobs. They often have not gotten their dream jobs, and they often have needed a lot of effort and persistence. But that's true of most people in the job market today.

We don't have a step-by-step program or checklist that we distribute to new members. Rather, we try to pass on a number of broader job search themes/lessons, drawn from our experiences since 2011. These are centered on accessing the resources available, functioning as a "helicopter family member," and joining other mutual support efforts in the local autism community.

1. Don't try to do it alone. Connect with the infrastructure of public and nonprofit placement agencies for adults with developmental differences, usually available at no cost: Nothing surprises us more than how many adults with autism and family members who come to the Club have no idea of the extensive infrastructure of public and nonprofit placement agencies available to them, usually at no cost. This was true in 2011 and remains true today.

Our main message to job seekers and their families is the following Don't do it alone; you don't need to. An infrastructure of employment services has grown up over the past four decades, and especially since the passage of the Americans with Disabilities Act (ADA) in 1990. You can't rely on this publicly-funded infrastructure; you need to take a lot of actions on your own. But it should be a central part of your job strategy.

In California, two large government departments exist to help place and retain adults with autism and other developmental differences: the California Department of Developmental Services (DDS) and the California Department of Rehabilitation (DOR). They provide employment services at no cost for adults who apply and are certified as having a disability.

DDS, with a budget of over $8.2 billion in 2019, funds and oversees a vast network of government and community-based agencies, serving over 333,000 youth and adults with developmental differences. These agencies are not limited to employment: they provide a wide range of housing, education, mental health, and supportive living services. But helping adults with developmental differences find and retain jobs is a main mission—given the wide agreement among DDS leadership on the central role of employment.

Job counselors funded by DDS start with an individualized employment plan for each adult and provide assistance in identifying and pursuing jobs. They or a separate job coach are available to help the adjustments to the workplace. All of these services are available at no cost to adults with developmental differences who qualify as DDS clients.

To qualify as a DDS client, an adult needs to show a "substantial disability" that began before the person's eighteenth birthday and is expected to continue indefinitely. For those adults with developmental differences who do not qualify, though, there are employment services through a separate state agency, DOR. These services also involve an individualized plan, assistance in finding and contacting potential employers, and on-the-job coaching to ensure retention. They also are available without cost.

The job counselors at both DDS and DOR usually have caseloads of over a hundred or even 150 adults, so their efforts need to be augmented, whenever possible, by family members and friends. But the counselors know the local job markets well, especially the employers who have hiring initiatives targeted at workers with developmental differences. They know the support that is usually needed on the job, at least for a time. We emphasize to new Club members: "You need to access these resources, even if the qualifying process can be frustrating and take some time."

For adults who do not qualify for either DDS or DOR, private job coaches are available. They can be retained individually by adults and/or family members.

2. For the job search process, be a "helicopter family member" constantly engaged in the job search and retention process, drawing on all contacts and resources to help: Most social messaging today is critical of family members, especially parents, who hover over and become too involved in their children's lives. What, if any, truth there might be in this criticism does not apply to the employment world for adults with developmental differences. Getting and holding a job today is far more difficult for all workers than in the past, and that includes workers with developmental differences.

We encourage family members to be in contact with the job counselor on strategies; to assist in the filing of applications online, which can be confusing for anyone; and to use whatever contacts they have in identifying job opportunities.

Following up on online job listings is worth doing—a few of our members have gotten jobs through the regular online processes with larger employers, like Amazon, CVS Pharmacies, and Starbucks. But as every job placement book today emphasizes, the main source of job leads is through networks of family, friends, and co-workers.

Family members will want to draw on all of their networks for job leads. They will also do so to carve out new job opportunities. A company can be convinced to add a worker with autism as that worker brings passion for an occupation or field, or brings specific skills or valued traits, such as regular attendance, loyalty, and focus. This is so especially as the company is able to access the wage subsidies and tax credits available for hiring adults with autism.

3. Reach out to the network of volunteer local autism groups: The Job Club is one type of mutual support. There are others associated with the community autism/disability groups, such as the chapters of the Autism Society, Autism Speaks, and Best Buddies, and local volunteer groups, such as Friends Like Me and the Shupin Independent Living in the Bay Area.

These groups practice mutual support centered on social networks and shared activities. Adults with autism and family come together for social activities and also to jointly address common issues of housing, public safety, and employment. Best Buddies, for example, started in the Bay Area primarily hosting social activities, dances, outings, and restaurant gatherings for its members. It has expanded to provide direct job placement and coaching, and to serve as a forum for participants to learn from each other about job search techniques and jobs available.

Part of why the mutual support groups are effective lies in how they incorporate four distinctive cultural elements of the autism community. First, all races and ethnic groups join together—there is none of the identity politics that have become part of other major institutions. Second, there is no ideology—liberal or conservative, Democrat or Republican, nobody cares. Third, nobody considers themselves a victim or socially oppressed. Fourth, adults with autism are regarded as active agents, involved in all activities and decision-making, rather than passive dependents.

***

THE JOB CLUBS and other mutual support entities do not need major government funding in the Act. The Act, though, will recognize the roles of the Clubs and other mutual support entities, and why autism employment cannot rely on government efforts and funding. The Act will also recognize the four elements of autism culture incorporated in the mutual support entities, and their importance.

7

"AUTISM FRIENDLY" WORKPLACE CULTURE

The main elements of the "autism friendly workplace" are set out. The processes for expanding these workplaces are discussed, as is the search for these workplaces by adults with autism and family members.

Assisting adults with autism with skills and behaviors to fit successfully into the workplace and workplace culture is the focus of most autism employment efforts today. But autism practitioners increasingly are seeking to alter workplace culture, to create an "autism friendly workplace," that can improve retention and reduce turnover.

Below we consider what is meant by "autism friendly workplace," how it has been implemented in recent years, and why it has not been more widely implemented.

Part I: The Elements of the "Autism Friendly Workplace"
The autism friendly workplace was briefly discussed in *The Autism Job Club* as a concept then beginning to gain currency in the 2014–2015 period among autism employment practitioners. Marcia Scheiner of Integrate was among the early advocates of addressing workplace

culture. At the time, the autism friendly workplace was mainly in the conceptual stage. Since that time, the Autism at Work companies and autism workforce consultancies have given fuller definition to its main elements, and put these elements into practice.

"Autism friendly workplace" is sometimes associated with physical elements, such as lighting or sound modifications or quiet spaces. These may be relevant in some cases, but they are not the main elements of the workplace cultural change envisioned. To a greater extent, autism friendly workplace has come to include five main elements:

- It is a workplace with supports for workers. These supports include mentors drawn from other workers at the company, supervisors and line managers with training in autism and developmental differences, and job coaches when needed.
- It is a workplace practicing patience in enabling workers to get up to speed. Workers are not fired for initial mistakes; they are given time to learn skills and adapt to workplace requirements.
- It is a workplace practicing flexibility in accepting certain behaviors that do not significantly disrupt the work process. Workers may laugh out loud, talk to themselves, repeat inappropriate phrases from television, or do a hundred other things that can be annoying. Supervisors and workplace mentors counsel them to be aware of the reactions of other workers. However, supervisors try to practice flexibility when unusual or odd behaviors do not undermine work processes.
- It is a workplace that doesn't focus on the negative, which is so often the case when adults with autism are hired. It recognizes the positive contributions that adults with autism frequently bring to the workplace environment, through perfect or near perfect attendance, gratitude for the job, and a positive attitude.

- It is a workplace with buy-in at all levels. The hiring of adults with autism and other developmental differences is recognized as of value by top officials and throughout the organization.

The employment initiatives at the Autism at Work and other major firms partnering with the autism consultancies are demonstrating that these elements are effective in reducing turnover. It is not that the hired adults with autism never run into difficulties at these firms. But the retention rates have been high. As Scheiner explains, the ethos of all of these elements is the employers and workers meeting halfway.

Part II: Expanding the Realm of the Autism Friendly Workplace

However, as noted in chapter 3, the number of the hiring initiatives among major firms, while growing, remains very small. Beyond these structured hiring initiatives, the elements of the autism friendly workplace have not been widely adopted.

Expanding the autism friendly workplace, like expanding the number of structured autism employment initiatives in private firms, starts with building on demonstrated effectiveness, and expanding on a firm-by-firm basis. There is not a workforce culture that is present across the American economy, and can be impacted.[1] Rather, there are hundreds of thousands of workplace cultures of individual businesses. These hundreds of thousands of business cultures can be reached not only by individual contacts, but also by a range of channels: industry associations, the public workforce system, social media, and the broader media.

Meristem, an autism consultancy and postsecondary program in Sacramento, recently completed content for an online training course related to the autism friendly workplace. The training is aimed at employers, with five modules of twenty minutes each on advantages of hiring adults with autism and best practices for incorporating these adults into the workforce. The Stanford Neurodiversity Project is completing its own employer training, on similar topics, but with shorter modules of five minutes each. Life Sherpa, Different Brains, and Autism Speaks are other consultancies undertaking broad outreach to employers, and media campaigns on autism hiring and the autism friendly workplace.

It will be a gradual process of expanding the autism friendly workplace culture, with each individual company success generating additional activity. Further, it will be a process that will require persistence—even at workplaces with individual managers and supervisors who are sympathetic to the autism friendly workplace.

Let me give a recent example from the San Francisco Public Utilities Commission (PUC), a local government agency that provides water to the County of San Francisco. The PUC oversees an expansive network of pumping stations, reservoirs, pipelines, and tunnels delivering water to over 2.7 million households and businesses. It employs an army of engineers, hydrologists, billing agents, maintenance staff, rate analysts, and chemists, over 2300 employees.

Masood Ordikhani, the PUC's workforce director, in early 2018 decided to expand the traditional diversity categories to include neurodiversity. "By 2018, the unemployment rate in San Francisco was under 2.5 percent, and we saw it as an opportunity to bring in workers who even in the booming economy were not finding jobs," Ordikhani later explained. "My staff reviewed the employment data, and adults with developmental disabilities in San Francisco stood out for their extremely high unemployment rate. At the same time, what I read and observed about workers with autism and other neurological conditions suggested that they could bring a lot to the PUC and our contractors in their empathy and untapped skills."[2]

Whether to disclose is an on-going issue in autism employment. The PUC program opted for full disclosure from the start, highlighting transparency, and letting other staff know about the participant coming on board and the program goals, and seeking to get buy-in from co-workers. Kristen Pedersen, the senior director of workforce inclusion at the Arc, which oversaw implementation, explains, "We sought support from all levels, supervisors and co-workers. Our experience is that as co-workers know about a person's developmental differences, they nearly always rally in support."[3]

I knew the worker with autism placed at the PUC in a provisional six month position, with the hope that it would lead into a regular civil service job, and some of the worker's past employment difficulties. After two months, though, when I hesitantly checked in on the worker's progress, Ordikhani was fully complimentary: "We're so lucky to have him. He brings such an upbeat nature to the job. Sometimes I'm down and I just need to see him to be picked up."

Ordikhani always focused on the positive, as well as patience and flexibility. Whenever we spoke, Ordikhani continued to say, "He's such an addition to our staff," and remark on the value he brought. Ordikhani observed how the worker advanced the program's understanding of autism. "He's the expert on autism." He added, "He teaches us about autism, so we can improve the program for future cycles."

Ordikhani further noted, "He's already had an impact on our workplace, making all of us more patient with each other, and recognizing how lucky we are to have these jobs." In one conversation, the issue of accommodations came up, and Ordikhani observed, "We all need accommodations, including me."

Yet, at the end of the provisional six month period, the worker was not moved into a regular civil service position, as hoped. The PUC was in the process of reducing office administration positions, including positions like mail room clerk, that previously might have been a fit. Further, despite Ordikhani's interest in neurodiversity, the PUC top leadership was willing to commit only to a work experience position, not an ongoing job.

A similar dynamic has been present with other employers, public and private. These employers have been willing to take on adults with autism for work experience for a set period, but not to subsequently hire these adults full time. Their commitment to the autism friendly workplace has been a partial one.

Part III: Finding Autism Friendly Workplaces

Adults with autism and family members will have central roles in this collective process of expanding autism friendly workforces across the economy. At the same time, in their own immediate job searches, they will want to look for workplaces that have at least some of the supports and ethos of the autism friendly workplace.

This is a point made by Donna D'Eri, an autism advocate and one of the founders of the autism focused business, The Rising Tide Car Wash. She tells Jennifer Palumbo of *Forbes*: "If you are someone who has a loved one who has autism and you're concerned about their career path, the D'Eri family recommends doing your research and looking for an environment with a great support system in place."[4]

The Autism at Work employers and employers connected to the autism consultancies have the most complete support systems and ethos. However, many other work environments have at least some of the supports and elements of the autism friendly workplace. Adults with autism and family members will want to seek these out.

Local non-profits and small businesses with someone with ties to the autism community are more likely to be supportive environments. Social services providers, profit and nonprofit, can be supportive environments—though not all are consistent in their own workplaces with what they preach. Nonprofits serving adults with autism and other developmental differences almost always are autism friendly workplaces themselves.

Goodwill operates a series of businesses employing adults with developmental differences along with its training programs. What has stood out to me for years about Goodwill is not only its supports, but also its emphasis on patience as an employer. William Rogers is the chief executive officer of Goodwill in the Bay Area, and he explains, "We are in the business of finding the right fit for each worker. This may take time, and it may take moving a worker to one or more different settings. But there's little point to what we're doing if we're not willing to be in this for the long run, for each individual worker."[5]

NOTES

1. In the 1970s, *The Greening of America* by Yale professor Charles Reich envisioned a new culture or consciousness among workplaces and the broader society. This consciousness (termed "Consciousness III" by Reich) would be one of voluntary cooperation, shunning competition, money and possessions, aiming at self-realization. This consciousness indeed was adopted by some individuals, but never on the social scale that Reich hoped for.
2. Masood Ordikhani, interview with author, July 2019.
3. Kristen Pedersen, interview with author, July 2019.
4. Jennifer Palumbo, "How One Company is Providing Jobs for Those with Autism," *Forbes*, September 8, 2020. https://www.forbes.com/sites/jennifer palumbo/2020/09/08/provide-jobs-for-those-with-autism/?sh =5b27857a10cf
5. William Rogers, interview with author, September 21, 2020.

8

AUTISM EMPLOYMENT IN STATE AND LOCAL GOVERNMENTS

State and local governments are major employers with more than twenty million jobs throughout the country. They regularly urge private employers to adopt hiring initiatives and create work environments for adults with developmental differences, but have failed to adopt and create these on any scale for themselves.

For years, state and local governments have encouraged private sector employers to hire adults with developmental differences. But these same governments, whose workforces totaled nearly 20.3 million workers at the end of 2020, have not hired and retained adults with autism and other developmental differences, on any scale.

Over the past decade, twenty-two states have issued executive orders and/or taken legislative actions under the State as Model Employer for workers with disabilities. These measures have set up an array of inter-agency task forces, working groups, advisory committees, and comprehensive plans for recruitment of workers with disabilities. They have established alternative processes to get on hiring lists and internships. They have introduced accessibility technology.[1]

Yet, most of these actions fall into the category of process rather than outcome. They have not led to significantly increased hiring, especially of workers with autism and developmental differences. California is one of the leading states set out as Model Employer, with a good number of the process actions, and its hiring outcomes have been modest.

Part I: Gap between Rhetoric of Disability Employment and Results in Government Jobs

The state of California is one of the largest employers in the nation, with 512,100 payroll jobs as of August 2020 (local governments in California combined had an additional 1,685,000 payroll jobs).

In the descriptions of the State as Model Employer disability initiatives, California is regularly singled out as an exemplar of disability hiring. In its 2017 report, "State as Model Employer Policies," the National Conference of State Legislatures highlights a series of actions taken by the state government of California as model actions.[2]

In 2002, the state legislature enacted a Workforce Inclusion Act, requiring a "comprehensive strategy" to bring workers with disabilities into state government employment. In 2005, Governor Arnold Schwarzenegger followed with an executive order directing state departments to review hiring practices to eliminate barriers to employment, to use "best efforts" in the recruitment hiring and advancement of workers with disabilities, and especially to make use of the Limited Examination and Appointment Program (LEAP). Schwarzenegger stated that "State government has an opportunity and a responsibility to lead by example, ensuring individuals with disabilities have an open door to the many opportunities in public service."[3]

Once more in 2010, Schwarzenegger issued an executive order requiring state agencies to strengthen their reasonable accommodations policies. In 2015, the State legislature enacted a new program of state internships for young adults with developmental disabilities, as a path to state employment.

The results of all of these efforts in terms of placements and retention have yet to be measured by a serious independent study. Practitioners who work with adults with developmental differences report few outcomes.

The LEAP program has been in existence since 1988, put forward as a way that workers with disabilities could get on hiring lists, if they met the posted qualifications for a position. The rationale: workers with disabilities would not be excluded by a written examination from jobs they would be able to do. But, over the years, LEAP has led to few hires. Getting on a hiring list has turned out to mean little.

Competition is considerable for nearly all state positions. Workers in California have figured out the obvious: for most jobs, the public sector pays more and has more benefits (especially health and retirement benefits) than private sector jobs. This is true especially for lower level clerical and administrative positions. Hiring managers in state government usually have tens (if not hundreds) of applicants on the hiring lists.

In 2015, Eric Nelson, a UC Davis statistician, reviewed the state data on LEAP and described the program, and more generally the employment of workers with disabilities in state government, as a "shell game."[4] Nelson claimed that between 1988 and 2013, more than half of the state's departments had made no LEAP hires. Further, to make their disability numbers look good, state departments instead had reclassified existing workers as "disabled." They reclassified older workers as "disabled," due to conditions linked to aging such as the onset of arthritis or the need for insulin.

Disability employment programs report no more than a handful of their clients hired through LEAP in the past few decades. Tom Heinz has been the executive director of East Bay Innovations (EBI) for the past twenty-six years, and has participated in the job searches of hundreds of adults with developmental disabilities. Repeatedly, he has tried without success to get clients into state government jobs, including through LEAP.

Heinz was one of the creators of the State Internship Program (SIP), beginning in 2014, to take a more aggressive approach to disability hiring. Heinz thought that by getting his clients into state employment as interns, hiring managers could see what the clients could do, and the internships could lead to full time civil service hiring. This was an approach that EBI had taken with other large employers, including PG&E, Kaiser Hospital, and Alameda County. "We knew no person with developmental disabilities who had been hired by LEAP, and thought by developing an internship for State employment that might make a difference."[5]

Heinz partnered in 2014 with another nonprofit, Futures Explored in the Sacramento area, and in 2015, SB644 was enacted by the state legislature. It established SIP under the state Department of Human Resources (CalHR) and provided for a partnership between the Department of Rehabilitation (DOR) and the Department of Developmental Services (DDS) to increase the number of young adults with developmental disabilities in State service.

In 2016, DOR staff began to contact state departments for placements. Over the next four years, DOR set out to engage hiring managers in the roughly 150 state departments, large and small, to take on interns, primarily in office administration assistance. The interns were of no cost to the departments; their wages covered by a wage subsidy program administered by DDS. Additionally, each intern came with a job coach, covered by DOR. Heinz and the DOR hoped for at least dozens of internships. However, by 2020 only twelve internships had been created.

Why so few? The SIP procedures, policies, and program regulations took over a year to be issued by CalHR, which stalled program momentum at the start. More importantly, once DOR staff started outreach, they soon found that hiring managers did not regard the interns, even at no cost, to be worth the extra effort in training and supervision. Michelle Alford-Williams, a former DOR manager for Workforce Development who was part of marketing SIP, recalls,

"Even with the full employee subsidies, the hiring managers could not fathom that individuals with developmental disabilities could do the jobs. Each internship took a long time to develop, and only a few departments participated."[6]

SIP has had initial success in moving the interns into regular civil service positions. Of the twelve interns, seven have been placed so far in regular civil service positions, as an office tech or office assistant. But even DOR officials, who champion the program, are disappointed with the very low numbers of hires, five years since SIP was enacted. "I and other senior managers at DOR have been involved in disability employment for decades, urging private employers to give our clients a chance, and we've been frustrated by the lack of job placements in our own state government," Alford-Williams observes.

Our AASCEND experiences with the disability initiatives in San Francisco City government have paralleled those in state government. The City has established its own Access to City Employment (ACE) program, providing an alternative route to city employment for individuals with developmental differences. It enables these individuals who meet the qualifications for a position to bypass the civil service testing structure and be reachable by the hiring manager.

Several of our AASCEND members have applied through the ACE process for entry level positions in offices, libraries, and parks and recreation, but none have been hired over the past five years. Like the California state LEAP program, the hiring decision in ACE is driven by the hiring manager in each department. Getting on a list guarantees nothing. Hiring managers in the city government, like those in state government, have more than enough applicants to choose from on hiring lists.

The city has also established a small internship program for young adults with developmental differences. But it serves mainly as work experience, not as a path into civil service employment.

Part II: Proven Hiring Model, Targeting Developmental Differences, and Setting Numerical Goals

Both the Council of State Governments (CSG) and the National Council of State Legislatures (NCSL) have issued reports in the past few years on the wide variety of State as Model Employer efforts among state governments.[7] The CSG divides the initiatives under Model Employer into six main categories: Formal mechanisms (executive orders, legislation) committing states to be model employers of workers with disabilities

- Infrastructure (cabinet positions, interagency task forces, working groups, and advisory committees)
- Comprehensive plans across state government
- Hiring goals and preferences
- Special appointment lists, trial work periods, paid internships

The NCSL list is similar in its categorization of the activities among statements of commitment, plans, goals, and special appointment lists.

What has been the impact of these activities? We can't say at this time. While there are descriptions of the activities undertaken in the NCSL and CSG reports, neither of these organizations has studied outcomes. Nor has any independent research body done so.[8] This is research that calls out to be undertaken, given the distance often between processes and outcomes. California shows that plans, task forces, and even the hiring lists and internships often do not translate into results.

However, we can begin to develop a strategy for increased hiring of adults with developmental differences in the public sector, by drawing on results discussed in earlier chapters with hiring initiatives in entities outside of the public sector. We can also draw on the results of the Section 503 federal program, which tried to set numerical guidelines for hiring by federal contractors.

Here are three approaches that are the start of a public sector hiring strategy.

The proven model of structured hiring/retention: The same model of targeted hiring and retention—designated job openings, job coaching and support networks, and buy-in from officials at all levels—that we've seen as a proven model in the private sector is applicable in the public sector. The State Internship Program in California was a disappointment in terms of the small numbers of internships. But its model of targeted hiring and retention did succeed in moving the interns into entry level administrative positions. DOR continues to strengthen the model, adding two elements: (i) regular contact by program staff with the participant's family and other support networks, and (ii) close tracking of individual progress.[9]

The proven model of workplace culture for retention: In a similar vein, the autism friendly workplace culture, applicable in private sector firms, is equally applicable in the public sector. This is the workplace culture (discussed in chapter 6) of patience, flexibility, and giving adults with developmental differences the time to learn skills; a workplace culture in which workers with developmental differences do not worry about being fired for the first inappropriate behavior.

In fact, a culture shift is even more needed in the public sector for hiring initiatives to succeed. Government workplaces often are more rigid and unwelcoming to workers with developmental differences than other workplaces, not less. This is true for the large structured and rule-bound Weberian bureaucracies that are present in many states, such as California—bureaucracies with thousands of employees. These bureaucracies benefit from a strong sense of professionalism. At the same time, their workforces can be highly territorial, with a considerable sense of job entitlement.

Hiring goals for workers with developmental differences and an enforcement mechanism: The majority of State as Model Employer initiatives usually reference "workers with disabilities." But this can be a very broad group, depending on how "disability" is defined. The LEAP experience in California suggests that departments can focus on those with relatively minor disabilities to meet hiring goals.

The Centers for Disease Control and Prevention (CDC) have defined disability broadly to include mobility disabilities that they claim affect one in seven adults. The CDC now estimates that one in four Americans (sixty-one million) have a disability that "impacts major life activities."[10] The Bureau of Labor Statistics (BLS) uses a more restrictive definition that is followed by most states. But the BLS definition still classifies over thirty million workers as having a disability in 2019.[11]

If adults with developmental differences are to be more fully included in state disability initiatives, the targeting of at least some of these initiatives needs to be specifically on them, not on disabilities more broadly. These initiatives should be limited to new hires, and exclude reclassification of the existing workforce.

The experience of the high profile federal disability initiative, Section 503 of the Rehabilitation Act of 1973, is instructive. In September 2013, the federal government added new requirements under Section 503 for federal contractors, setting a goal that at least 7 percent of the contractor workforce be workers with disabilities.

A survey of 235 federal contractors by the Institute on Employment and Disability at Cornell University after the first three years of implementation found greater awareness of setting targets/goals around recruitment and hiring and greater self-identification by existing workers.[12] But only 30 percent of the respondents agreed with the statement that the Section 503 regulations "will lead to increased employment of people with disabilities in my organization." The survey did not try to capture numbers of new hires.

Further, as the implementation of Section 503 has come into view, practitioners and advocates in the developmental disability field have been critical, pointing out two shortcomings of the Section 503 regulations. First, Section 503 lacks an enforcement mechanism: it has no clear consequences for contractors who fail to meet the 7 percent goal. Second, it utilizes the broad definition of disabilities and allows companies to meet the 7 percent goal with reclassifications of their existing workforces.

Mark Erlichman, the deputy director at DOR with over thirty years of experience in the field, argues that change in state hiring of workers with developmental differences is likely to come only with stricter hiring goals for government departments. "Observing state hiring or non-hiring of workers with disabilities for over three decades, I have concluded that something needs to change, and it would be a mix of hiring requirements for departments and funding to departments for supports," he says.[13]

Michelle Alford-Williams recalls being on a state task force in California in 2015 in which the setting of numerical goals in state hiring was put forward by the Association of California State Employees with Disabilities. The recommendation to set numerical goals for workers with disabilities was adopted by the task force, but never implemented by the state human resources agency. Alford-Williams has come to believe that numerical goals need to be set more narrowly for workers with developmental disabilities, and that some enforcement mechanism is needed. She says, "My experience over three decades is that the broad category of disabilities is not enough for achieving outcomes in hiring workers with developmental disabilities, and that some budget consequences need to be included in cases where departments consistently do not meet these goals."

***

STATE AND LOCAL governments operate within civil service processes that are not easily changed, and the public sector, operating outside of the market economy, is usually slow to move. But it is precisely because the public sector is not under the market pressures of the private sector that it, like the universities, nonprofits, and private foundations singled out in chapter 3, has greater flexibility in and rationale for the hiring of adults with developmental disabilities.

NOTES

1. The Council of State Governments, "State as a Model Employer," February 2017, https://seed.csg.org/tag/state-as-a-model-employer/.
2. National Conference of State Legislatures, "State as Model Employer Policies," 2017, https://www.ncsl.org/research/labor-and-employment/state-as-model-employer-policies.aspx.
3. Ibid.
4. Eric L. Nelson, "Disability Counts & The State's Shell Game," *Trends in State Work*, 2015, http://trendsinstatework.blogspot.com/2015/05/disability-counts-states-shell-game.html.
5. Tom Heinz, e-mail to author, August 14, 2020.
6. Michelle Alford-Williams, interview with author, December 28, 2020.
7. National Conference of State Legislatures, "State as Model Employer Policies", 2017, https://www.ncsl.org/research/labor-and-employment/state-as-model-employer-policies.aspx.
8. The Federal government has its own special appointment process known as Schedule A. It allows workers with disabilities to apply for a federal positon through an alternative hiring process, if they meet the qualifications for the position. Like the state alternative hiring processes, though, Schedule A has yet to be subject to critical study.
9. DOR has strengthened employment supports and tracking. The new twenty-five-page Student Internship Program Notebook sets out a duty statement and training plan for each participant, in-person coaching as needed, and at least three progress reports over the 510 hours of the internship.
10. Centers for Disease Control and Prevention, "CDC: 1 in 4 US Adults Live with A Disability," August 16, 2018. https://www.cdc.gov/media/releases/2018/p0816-disability.html.
11. US Bureau of Labor Statistics, "Persons with a Disability: Labor Force Characteristics—2019," Washington, DC, February 2020, https://www.bls.gov/news.release/disabl.htm.

12. Sarah von Schrader & Susanne Bruyere, "What Works? How Federal Contractors are Implementing Section 503," Cornell University, 2018, https://ecommons.cornell.edu/bitstream/handle/1813/90120/DE _Section503_ReportFinal.pdf?sequence=1&isAllowed=y.
13. Mark Erlichman, interview with author, August 17, 2020.

9

PROFESSIONALIZING THE DIRECT SUPPORT WORKFORCE

The Direct Support Workforce forms the front lines of services, including employment services, in the disability field. A movement is underway to professionalize this workforce and recognize the work as a craft. The movement and the relation to craft are considered.

Eric Zigman, the director of the Golden Gate Regional Center, has been involved in employment programs for adults with developmental differences for over thirty years. In May 2019, at a hearing of the California state legislature, he spoke of the importance of the direct support workforce—the job developers, case managers, job coaches, and independent living coaches—in the success of these programs:

> In my experience there is no more important relationship in the Lanterman Act service system (for adults with developmental differences) than the relationship between the person served and the person directly serving them. All our grand plans for service design, quality assurance, monitoring and

accountability, do not amount to a "hill of beans" if the relationship between the Direct Support Professional (DSP) and the individuals receiving the support is not a quality relationship that can be sustained, consistently over time.[1]

Zigman is part of an effort in California and nationwide to professionalize this direct support workforce: to see it as a craft, to ensure a high quality of services through identifying the knowledge and skills associated with these services, establishing training and certifications, and tying increased wage levels to expertise and experience. The effort has enlisted practitioners throughout the nation as well as a number of national disability organizations.

Part I: The Craft of the Direct Support Workforce

In popular movies and novels about autism, the direct support workforce—support aides in education, residential homes, independent living, and employment—are presented in a positive light. In *Rain Man*, Ray's aide Vern is protective of Ray and flexible with Ray's rules. "Ray, my main man" says Vern, as he calms Ray after Charlie touches Ray's books.

In *The Curious Incident of the Dog in the Night-Time*, Christopher's aide Siobhan encourages Christopher with his book, and encourages him to take his Math A-Level exams. In the BBC television series, *The A Word*, Joe's aide Terry stands up for Joe's inclusion in a regular school.

Among our AASCEND members, the experiences with support aides have been near uniformly positive. This is true of independent living coaches provided by the Regional Center and job coaches provided by the Regional Center and by the Department of Rehabilitation. Coaches are described as supportive, empathetic, and "on my side." Devon is currently a job coach for one of our AASCEND members, James. He comes to the job site and assists James in learning the required job skills (and is able to step in and help resolve any work issues that might arise). He's always positive about James.

Though the current direct support system is by no means a dysfunctional one, Zigman and other disability agency leadership believe it can function better. Their vision is of direct support employment that is a profession and a craft: not a job that people fall into and do for a time until they find something better.

The craft of direct support jobs includes several values: empathy for the clients served and their goals, understanding these goals to serve at times as translator or facilitator, and knowing how to address behaviors that get in the way of these goals. Craft for the direct support workforce also includes some of the more general values of craft: attention to detail, willingness to invest time in a task to get it right, and integrity.

Zigman uses Creativity Explored as an example:

We have a community-based program, Creativity Explored, that assists adults with developmental differences in arts projects. It is mainly an avocational rather than vocational program, though participants do sell their products on eBay and other websites. The support staff, a number of whom have been there many years, take very seriously their role in helping participants and take very seriously the art of the participants. It is not just another job for them.

I see in the direct support workforce at Creativity Explored and their sense of mission part of the model for other settings. The workforce stands out in its stability, and lower turnover than other settings.

Building a direct support workforce of craftpersons is rooted in stability. There is the value of stability in the craftsperson's longterm involvement in the field, and there is the value in stability in each relation with the individual receiving support.[2]

Several reports in recent years on direct support workers have zeroed in on the lack of stability and tying the lack of stability to wage levels.

The President's Committee for People with Intellectual Disabilities entitled its 2017 report, "America's Direct Support Workforce Crisis."[3] The report described a workforce nationwide with average DSP wages of $10.72 per hour, many DSPs working two or three jobs, and the average annual DSP turnover rates drawn from several other studies of 45 percent. Given the range of costs among the states, it stopped short of calling for a specific national wage rate, but did urge disability agencies to reduce turnover by recognizing "sufficient DSP wages and compensation packages."

In its 2018 annual Staff Stability Survey, the National Association of State Directors of Developmental Disability Services reported an alarming 51.3 percent turnover rate for the year among 331,512 direct support professional (DSP) positions of its member agencies.[4] In 2019, the budget study commissioned by the California state legislature noted similar high turnover, and estimated that direct support wages needed to be increased by 20–30 percent in most areas of the state to find and hold the desired workforce.[5]

Ask community providers about how to improve service quality, and reducing turnover among direct support workforce comes up right away.[6] "We have had a difficult time holding on to our direct employment staff," explains Vic Wursten, senior vice president at Pride Industries, based outside of Sacramento. Pride is among the largest providers nationwide of employment services for adults with developmental disabilities. Pride serves roughly 1300 adults each year, with around 650 adults employed in its business enterprises (product fulfillment, sorting/packing, and logistics), 400 placed in businesses outside of Pride, and 250 in day program activities. Pride employs a staff of 135 direct support professionals.[7]

Wursten adds:

> The rate that we are able to pay direct support professionals
> is based on the reimbursement rates from the state. In recent
> years we have been able to pay only slightly above minimum

wage for our production trainers and job coaches. Minimum wage in Sacramento County is now $13.50 and we're able to pay our production trainers and job coaches $14.75. We're able to pay our case managers a little higher, at $21 an hour and job developers at $22 an hour. But we've had to convert them to hourly workers, where they previously were on salary.[8]

Part II: Wage Rates, Credentials, Advancement, and Building the DSP Craft

There's a reason, of course, that the DSP wages have been slow to increase, especially by state governments. Even modest increases are expensive. In California, a minimum wage increase of one dollar that took effect in January 2020 (raising the minimum wage from twelve to thirteen dollars per hour) is projected to cost over $194 million in increases to DSPs just in the next fiscal year.[9] Further, the $194 million does not include a wage increase for workers in counties, like Los Angeles and the Bay Area counties, whose minimum wage is already above the thirteen dollars per hour state level.

In recent years, the national disability groups have turned to the federal government, urging the federal government to increase rates for DSP services through the Medicaid system. They have accompanied their advocacy with efforts to build DSP as a craft: through recognition of DSPs in the US Department of Labor occupation system, establishment of a series of DSP credentialing requirements, and expansion of career mobility for DSPs within their field.

In March 2020, Senators Maggie Hassan and Susan Collins introduced the Recognizing the Role of Direct Support Professionals Act, which directs that the federal government in its Standard Occupational Classification system establish a new code for the DSP, recognizing it as a profession. The change is meant as a first step toward fuller data on workforce shortage areas and toward identifying the valued skills and advancement paths.

For job counselors, for example, valued skills would be ones related to employer outreach, job search techniques, and local labor markets. For job coaches, these skills would be ones related to workforce retention strategies and to the mental health issues and comorbidities that often undermine employment of adults with developmental differences.

"As the mother of a son who experiences severe disabilities, I know firsthand what a difference Direct Support Professionals can make in the lives of those they work with," Senator Hassan said in introducing the bill. "We need more Direct Support Professionals in the workforce who can provide such critical, high quality care."[10]

Both tied to and beyond this Act, several national disability groups are developing a system of credentialing as a foundation for wage increases and advancements. The National Alliance of Direct Support Professionals (NADSP) is one of the most active. It proposed in a 2019 report, "Moving from Crisis to Stabilization: The Case for Professionalizing the Direct Support Workforce Through Credentialing," a series of skills demonstrations/credentials (DSP Level 1, DSP Level 2, DSP Level 3) that could be integrated into a state's reimbursement rate schedule.[11] Tying wages to credentials, the report authors argued, would bring increased tenures, a path for career advancement, and most of all, improved quality of support.

Nicole Jorwic, the senior director of Public Policy for The Arc of the United States, was one of the national disability officials who testified at a November 2019 Congressional hearing on the direct care "crisis" in disability services. She stated: "In my role at the Arc I am lucky to spend a fair amount of my time on the road speaking and meeting with our (more than 600) chapters, families and individuals with disabilities. Nearly everywhere I go, the number one issue that I hear about most is the workforce crisis when it comes to serving individuals with disabilities."[12]

She went on to single out the low wages and high turnover rates, adding, "the word 'crisis' doesn't really do it justice—having a skilled properly trained and fairly paid workforce is the linchpin for success for so many people with disabilities to live the independent life that they choose." She spoke about her own brother, Chris, thirty, a person with autism and the turnover in DSPs that he has been experiencing.

"Chris has DSPs who come throughout the week to get Chris out into the community, he spends time volunteering with the elderly, working out and exploring job opportunities. It sounds great, right? And it can be, but it all hangs on a thread, in my home state of Illinois where the average DSP is even lower at under $10 per hour, a very thin thread."[13]

Earlier in the fall, Chris's main DSP had quit. It was two months later and a new DSP had not been hired, so Chris's services had been reduced to three days a week for less than six hours.

Jorvic went on to urge federal funding to support DSP wages as the most direct way to make a significant impact in reducing turnover. She too linked wages to demonstration of skills through credentialing and mobility.

***

THE AUTISM FULL Employment Act will want to build on these efforts to reduce turnover and tie wage increases to skills and experience. It will do so around the organizing principle of craft.

Additional Note: Direct Support Work as First Job for Aspiring Policymakers

There is a further benefit of approaching any direct support workforce reforms in terms of the concept of craft. Aspiring policymakers in the disability and related fields would be encouraged, if not expected, to start their careers as direct support workers. There is no better training for anyone who aspires to leadership or policy positions with community providers, government, nonprofits, or foundations than to spend at least five years as a direct support worker. It is really the only way to understand the field.

NOTES

1. Eric Zigman, "Panel Remarks for Senate Sub 3: Provider Rate Study and New Rate Setting Methodology," Sacramento, May 9, 2019.
2. Eric Zigman, interview with author, August 27, 2020.
3. President's Committee for People with Intellectual Disabilities, "Report to the President: America's Direct Support Workforce Crisis," Washington, DC, 2017, https://nadsp.org/report-to-the-president-2017/.
4. National Association of State Directors of Developmental Disabilities Services, "National Core Indicators: Staff Stability Survey Report," 2018, https://www.nasddds.org/projects/national-core-indicators/.
5. The consultants, Burns and Associates, surveyed over 1100 providers throughout the state, as well as 1700 clients and family members, looking into turnover and wages. Burns & Associates, "DDS Vendor Rate Study and Rate Models," Sacramento, California, March 15, 2019. http://www.harborrc.org/files/uploads/DDS_Vendor_Rate_Study_Report_Released_03-15-19.pdf.
6. Community Mainstreaming, "The Direct Support Professional Crisis", https://communitymainstreaming.org/the-direct-support-professional-crisis/ (retrieved August 2020); Nancy Cutler, "Low pay feeds shortage of workers who care for people with developmental disabilities," northjersey.com, May 28, 2019; Lynn Hetzler, "Behind the Poor Pay and High Turnover Rates of Direct Support Professionals," *Relias*, June 16, 2016.
7. Pride employs fifteen job developers and seventy-five job coaches for the outside job placements, and twenty-two case managers and sixty production trainers for its own businesses.
8. Vic Wursten, interview with author, October 19, 2020.
9. California Department of Developmental Services, "Regional Centers, May 2020 Revision," Sacramento, California, May 2020, https://www.dds.ca.gov/wp-content/uploads/2020/05/2020_2021_RC_DCMayRevision.pdf#page=198.
10. Maggie Hassan, Press Release of the Office of Senator Maggie Hassan, March 2, 2020, https://www.hassan.senate.gov/news/press-releases/senators-hassan-collins-introduce-bipartisan-legislation-to-help-address-critical-need-for-more-direct-support-professionals.

11. D. Smith, J. Macbeth, C. Bailey, "Moving from Crisis to Stabilization: The Case for Professonalizing the Direct Support Workforce Through Credentialing," NADSP, Albany, New York, February 2019.

12. Nicole Jorwic, Testimony to Congressional Hearing on "The Hidden Crisis of Care in the United States," November 1, 2019.

13. Nicole Jorwic, "Congressional Testimony: The Direct Care Crisis," November 1, 2019, https://thearc.org/congressional-testimony-the-direct-care-crisis/.

10

AUTISM-FOCUSED BUSINESSES

The autism-focused businesses represent a niche market for autism employment, but an important one. The growth of this market lies in the autism community itself, though the Act will contribute in several ways.

The pandemic halted the growth of most of the main autism-focused businesses. But these businesses, arising during the past decade and forming a niche market of employment, have not gone out of operation. They look to grow again during the recovery, and be joined by other autism-focused businesses.

The growth of these businesses is rooted in the autism community itself: the current businesses assisting startups, investment by members of the autism community who are in position to do so, and utilization or promotion of these business services by autism advocates and allies. But like other social ventures, which they resemble, these businesses often operate with little financial security, as they balance goals of targeted hiring and retention with business competition. The Act will consider contracting opportunities and financial supports for these businesses.

Part I: The Autism-Focused Businesses Today

The term autism-focused business refers to a business that has a core mission of employing adults with autism. Though there is no registry or official count of these businesses, a rough survey finds at least forty that are active and employing at least five workers.

A number of the businesses are in low tech fields, such as a car wash (Rising Tide) and an artisan chocolate company (The Chocolate Spectrum). Others, such as Ultranauts, Aspiritech, and Daivergent, employ adults with autism in more tech-oriented software engineering and data analytics services. Ventures ATL is a mix, creating jobs for adults in the middle range of complexity and technology acumen by operating businesses in both data management and product fulfillment.

Nearly all of the businesses have been launched by parents and family members. A main goal has been to employ family members and others in the local autism community who have had difficulty finding employment in mainstream settings. Family members have left stable employment and/or professional positions to work full time on these ventures.

The growth of these companies says a lot about the lengths that family members will go to ensure employment. It says a lot about the importance they see in employment in the lives of their family members.

The business founders also speak of the meaning they find in their enterprises. They recognize that the number of direct hires is small, but see themselves as adding to the knowledge base of better autism policy. George Eliot writes of Dr. Lydgate in *Middlemarch*: "He was ambitious of a wider effect, he was fired with the possibility that he might work out the proof of an anatomical conception, and make a link in the chain of discovery."[1] A similar description might be given to these business founders.

Rising Tide Car Wash, Ultranauts, Daivergent, and Ventures ATL are four of the most successful autism-focused businesses. They indicate what is possible: skills that the founders are bringing to their businesses and how these businesses are growing. As we listen to the founders speak, we hear their commitment and idealism.

Rising Tide Car Wash: The Rising Tide Car Wash is perhaps the best-known of the autism-focused businesses. Started in April 2013 by John D'Eri, whose son Andrew is an adult with autism, it grew rapidly to employ thirty-five adults by 2014.[2] D'Eri became a national presence, appearing on the NBC *Nightly News* and presenting a TED talk.

He candidly spoke in 2014 of what drove him and his family to start the car wash, even though they had no experience in the car wash field: "When I thought of Andrew, I could not see an independent man at age forty. Instead, I could only see him living at home, with no sense of purpose, no friends, no social ties."[3]

Reviewing the employment landscape for Andrew and other adults with autism, D'Eri added, "Although a vibrant, lighthearted young man, Andrew's disability is a clear competitive disadvantage when it comes to securing gainful employment. We believe that Andrew and others like him have difficulty getting a job, not because they don't have the tools to be top-notch employees, but rather because most businesses are simply not structured in a way that allows them to reach their full potential."

By 2020, Rising Tide employs around seventy-five adults with autism (along with twenty or so other workers) between its original Parkland, Florida location and a second car wash in Margate, Florida. Andrew's role is as a Driver's Side Associate and Donna D'Eri told *Forbes*:

> He is delighted with his work—even in these times during the pandemic where he has to wear a mask and wash his hands more often, not to mention the heat. He never complains and seems to really like working with his teammates and having his own money. He gets so much more from his job than he can verbally express.[4]

Rising Tide is now in the process of developing a third location in South Florida. Tom D'Eri states: "Both of our locations achieve high marks against industry averages in most key performance areas such as sales volume, customer satisfaction, and service speed because of how well our team works together."[5]

Ultranauts: Ultanauts provides data engineering services to large companies. Founded in 2013 by Rajesh Anandan and Art Shectman, two MIT-trained engineers, it initially focused on basic software testing. Like other autism-focused business start-ups of that time, including Specialist Guild and Semperical, Ultranauts saw software testing as a fit for the heightened abilities among adults with autism in focus, attention to detail, and natural pattern recognition. These other autism-focused software testing start-ups were not able to survive as the basic software testing market moved overseas. Ultranauts proved able to pivot and move into higher-end data quality and software quality engineering services.

Anandan is one of the few founders who does not have a direct family member who is an adult with autism. He traces his passion for autism employment to his wife, a clinical psychologist, who has worked with children with autism. In her experience, the strengths of these children were often overlooked by educators, who too often focused on weaknesses.[6]

In his client presentations, Anandan places the emphasis on the quality of service provided by Ultranauts, rather than the social mission of employing adults with autism. "Ultranauts provides quality engineering and assurance services to a wide range of Fortune 500 enterprises, hyper-growth start-ups and top-tier digital consultancies," the company presentation begins, and goes on to list some of the large firms that Ultranauts provides engineering services to: AIG, Cigna, Prudential, T-Mobile, BNYMellon, and Warner Media.

The case studies presented by Anandan are framed not in terms of the employment of adults with autism, but how Ultranauts has outperformed other mainstream software engineering companies. In one case study involving software testing for Prudential, Anandan explains that "Ultranauts increased bug detection by 56% versus the previous vendor, which was IBM." In another, involving end-to-end test automation for BNY Mellon, Ultranauts "helped client automate over a dozen applications and achieve several million dollars in cost savings."[7]

By mid-2020, Ultranauts has grown to seventy-five employees, of whom roughly three-quarters are adults with autism. It benefited in August 2019 from a financing round that brought in $3.5 million in new investments. Its model from the start has utilized a remote workforce (spread among twenty states), so it was well-situated when the pandemic arrived, and plans to expand following the pandemic.

One of Anandan's themes when he talks to general audiences about autism employment is that Ultranauts' success is due in good part to its "cognitively diverse" workforce.[8] The theme is in line with claims by some business theorists in recent years that teams are better at problem solving when they are diverse in terms of information processing styles.[9] The evidence for this remains limited, though, and more research remains to be undertaken at Ultranauts and other firms highlighting neurodiversity.

Daivergent: Daivergent is the brainchild of Byran Dai, trained as a data scientist at Harvard and Johns Hopkins. He founded the data labeling and work readiness company in December 2017 at age twenty-eight, with a former classmate and data engineer Rahul Mahida. As Dai often explains, he was motivated by his younger brother Brandon, a person with autism, who he worried would not find a place in the job world. He describes his brother as able to perform "detail-oriented, complex, repetitive kinds of work that form the data structure of artificial intelligence and machine learning."[10] He saw data labeling as a promising area for other adults with autism.

Dai launched the company with fifty thousand dollars of his own savings, and worked out of his apartment for the first year. In November 2018, the company obtained $950,000 in outside investment that enabled it to significantly expand its marketing to firms with data labeling needs and to expand its pool of candidates.

Daivergent has a team of eleven staff members, of which half are core employees based in New York City. The team pushes the data labeling assignments out to adults with autism around the country. As Dai explains, "Our goal is to enable adults with autism who have the interest and skills to work in the twenty-first century economy to take on projects for pay, build a portfolio, and move into a career in data and beyond."[11]

According to Dai, by late 2020, since its founding, Daivergent had provided paid work to over 520 adults, and had over two thousand users registered on its platform. As Daivergent wins data labeling projects, it offers the project work to these candidates, while ensuring the quality of work output. The Daivergent technology platform is able to connect candidates to opportunities by assessing users for their data labeling abilities and matching them to the projects which are the best fit.

In the post pandemic economy, Dai is looking not only to expand the project opportunities for the workers on its platform, but also to evolve into a sourcing pipeline of workers with autism into remote full time and part-time jobs.

To this end, Daivergent is now reaching out to firms with data labeling needs to identify employment opportunities as well as project work. "I see Daivergent as broadening into a full service platform for adults with autism interested in jobs that can be done from home," he says. "These adults can start with project work to build up their resume, take assessments to demonstrate their capabilities, and ultimately move into jobs that match their aspirations. The ties we are developing with companies needing data labeling will help us achieve this, as these companies are always looking for great talent across the United States."

Ventures ATL: Ventures ATL, based in Atlanta, operates two separate business ventures: product fulfillment and data entry. Its founders, the husband-wife team of Chet Hurwitz and Sara Barron, are hoping to add to their portfolio of small businesses, providing diverse employment opportunities.

Hurwitz is an attorney and former PwC partner and IBM executive with more than thirty-five years of experience, working with businesses large and small. In September 2011, when his son David, an adult with autism, was twenty, Hurwitz became a board member of Aspiritech, one of the early autism-focused businesses in software testing. He used his own resources to travel and recruit customers for Aspiritech. In 2016, he and Barron, a former marketing director, decided to commit full time to developing and operating autism-focused businesses. In May 2017 they launched their first business in data management, employing two adults with autism, and the following month started a second business in product fulfillment.

Like the other businesses, Ventures ATL emphasizes the quality service provided, rather than the social mission of hiring adults with autism. Hurwitz has described his marketing approach as focusing on "the business case: a cost effective and on demand domestic resource providing high quality service in areas where good performers are hard to find and retain."[12]

Keystone Insurers Group has become one of the major clients of the Ventures ATL data management services as excellent performance has led to a broader service relationship. One of the first projects involved assisting Keystone in the transition from a legacy database to a new Salesforce-based database. The project involved matching accounts between the two databases so that an account's data in the legacy database could be transferred into the correct account in the new database.

Keystone praised Ventures ATL for its completion of the project with high accuracy and under budget, and has steadily increased the workflow to Ventures ATL in a number of mission-critical areas with tight delivery timelines. Ventures ATL has developed data management clients in other industries (commercial real estate and professional/consulting services) while demonstrating that its employees can perform some more-nuanced tasks that require a moderate level of research and analytical skills.

During the pandemic, Ventures ATL has kept both its product fulfillment and data businesses in operation while migrating to a remote working model. The pace of new client acquisition has slowed and some client projects have been placed on hold. Nonetheless, Ventures ATL has now grown its employee headcount to fourteen employees while investing in new skill development for its employees (coding/SQL) as well as industry specific credentials (HIPAA for healthcare clients).

Part II: Growing the Autism-Focused Businesses

The expansion of the autism-focused businesses going forward in 2021 will start with mutual support in the autism community: the recruitment and training of new entrepreneurs, the sharing of expertise and resources among autism-focused existing businesses and start-ups, the community investment, and the utilization and promotion of services and products.

"Most of the people I've come across who are interested in starting autism-focused businesses are 'reluctant entrepreneurs' who have jumped into the entrepreneurial life due to a perceived necessity in order to support their loved ones with autism," observes Tom D'Eri. "Most of them are in their fifties and are taking action because their children with autism have grown into adults and have very limited or no job opportunities . . . There is a need to surround these aspiring entrepreneurs with resources such as entrepreneurial education, mentors, and seed funding." [13]

D'Eri urges that more siblings of individuals with autism become involved in these businesses: "Siblings in their twenties generally have much lower personal overheads and a long enough time horizon, make mistakes and grow businesses. In my opinion the best way to stoke the interest of siblings is to communicate and show that starting autism-focused businesses is not 'charity,' rather it's a legitimate way to build a successful life and make your mark on the world."

D'Eri and his family have started Rising Tide U, a training program for family members and others who have heard of Rising Tide and want to start autism-focused businesses. He says, "We've had students who have founded a variety of businesses including a film studio (Adapt Labs), a dog treat business (Brady's Biscuits), an artisanal goods business (Aspire Accessories), and several pizza concepts. All together our students have started about twenty businesses and are employing over a hundred individuals."

Hurwitz and Barron of Ventures ATL also are contacted regularly from others in the autism community who have business ideas—a coffee shop, a computer recycling center, a scanning business, to name a few in the past months. "We hear from other people who share our concern for the employment gap and hope to make a difference in their own communities," Barron notes. They are documenting their experiences and lessons learned for aspiring businesses.

As Hurwitz explains, "We received invaluable insights from [a] variety of autism focused businesses prior to starting Ventures ATL and we want to do the same for others who are considering new enterprises." Hurwitz believes that in many cases the most valuable insight they can offer is how to approach these enterprises from a business perspective, adding "the strong desire to create an autism-focused business cannot diminish the focus on the critical financial and operational success factors."

Autism employment advocates are establishing investment funds. One of our AASCEND members, Bay Area venture capitalist Brian Jacobs, established Moai Capital (after the giant hand-carved Moai statues on Easter Island) targeting investments in companies employing adults with autism. He is an investor in Ultranauts and Daivergent. Other funders in these two companies are the Disability Opportunity Fund and SustainVC, one of the emerging networks of venture capital funds targeting companies with social missions.

Each of the four autism-focused businesses noted above emphasizes its quality of services. But for all, their marketing has benefited from their mission in employing adults with autism. They are tapping into the market of individuals and companies who agree with this mission—either as they have family or friend connections or as ideological allies. The demographics of autism are increasing this market for mutual support and will continue to do so.

Beyond such mutual support, are there public policies that can expand the autism-focused businesses? To answer this, we must put the autism-focused businesses in the context of the broader movement of social enterprises. Like the autism-focused businesses, the social enterprises have dual goals: providing goods or services for purchase, and targeting the employment of individuals with the greatest difficulties in finding steady work.

Over the past four decades, hundreds of social enterprises have been launched, targeting the employment of ex-offenders, at-risk youth, and ex-addicts, as well as adults with disabilities. The enterprises have been in landscaping, construction, cleaning and maintenance, and food preparation to name a few of the main fields. In the majority of cases, the businesses have required subsidies, often generous subsidies, to stay in the market place. Many have ceased operations when subsidies ended or when the entrepreneurial founders have moved on.

Despite this mixed economic record, the social-enterprise movement is very much alive today. At the center of this movement is REDF, an organization founded in 1997 by George R. Roberts of the private equity investment firm, KKR & Co, and generously supported over the years by Roberts. REDF provides capital, relationship building, and marketing/strategy to social enterprises, and since 1997 has invested in more than a hundred social enterprises in twenty-one states.[14] The social enterprises are meant mainly as transitional employment, to help the most-challenged workers to gain a foothold and move onto employment in the mainstream economy.[15]

Carla Javits has been the president and CEO of REDF since 2007, and is a leading proponent of the social enterprise/transitional employment approach as a highly cost-effective employment approach. In a recent presentation, she pointed to data on the sharp decrease in government benefits among workers hired by the REDF-funded social enterprises. Prior to being hired, workers reported that 71 percent of their income came from government (food stamps, welfare), and 25 percent reported that they had not held a job. After social enterprise employment, the reliance on government benefits dropped to 24 percent.[16]

Javits knows firsthand of the substantial efforts and resources needed to keep each individual social enterprise in operation. She has searched in recent years for a better system of scaling and sustainability. To this end, REDF is pursuing a greater role in government contracting for social enterprises as well as a greater role in capital access funds.

Government contracting: Since the 1970s, the federal government has sponsored a program, AbilityOne, that promotes federal agency purchasing from nonprofit agencies that employ workers who are blind or have a significant disability—these workers must receive at least 75 percent of the direct labor hours performed by the enterprise. In 2020, federal government agencies purchased $3.6 billion of good and services from over five hundred nonprofits. AbilityOne was authored by Ms. Javits' father, the late Senator Jacob Javits (the Javits-Wagner-O'Day Act of 1971).[17]

AbilityOne has come under sharp criticism in recent years from disability groups and from the National Council on Disability, for the declining number of workers in the program, the limited percentage of revenue going to pay wages for people who are blind or have a significant disability (down from 20.09 percent to 18.19 percent between FY2011 and FY2018), and the employment of workers for less than minimum wage, based on companies utilizing 14c certificates. In an October 2020 report, the National Council on Disability called for a major revamp of the program to end the dominance of the program by nonprofits that had long-term, nonecompetitive agreements and to end the subminimum wage, among other changes.[18]

A restructuring of the AbilityOne program and contracting with the federal government will be coming soon. It provides an opportunity for autism-focused businesses, like other social ventures, to consider how revised federal contracting rules can benefit the network of autism-focused business. The autism-focused businesses currently all pay at least minimum wage, offer integrated settings, and should be very competitive in any open competition.[19]

Capital access and Wage Subsidies: REDF's 2021 national policy agenda prioritizes capital access for social enterprises. It seeks to include social enterprises as eligible for investment under the Community Economic Development grants and Job Opportunities for Low Income Individuals grants (as administered by the Department of Health and Human Services), and to reinstate the Corporation for National and Community Service Social Innovation Fund.[20]

REDF also has developed a 2021 policy agenda for state level actions. Chief among these is linking social enterprises to the existing WIOA work experience and on-the-job training funds.

For any of the autism-focused businesses, these three REDF social enterprise strategies may or may not be applicable. As a group, though, the autism-focused businesses will want to connect with the social enterprise movement, with whom they share a market-based approach.

***

THE AUTISM-FOCUSED BUSINESSES require such extraordinary commitment by their entrepreneurs that they will always be a niche employment venue. But their importance is beyond their number of direct hires. They demonstrate the importance that the autism community attaches to employment. They provide examples of a positive workplace culture for adults with autism and other developmental differences.

NOTES

1. George Eliot, *Middlemarch,* New York, New American Library, 1964.
2. Chapter 14 of *The Autism Job Club* briefly discussed Rising Tide, then less than two years old, as having an uncertain future. In the years since, it has not only survived, but expanded.
3. John D'Eri, "Rising Pride," TED talk, April 16, 2014.
4. Jennifer Palumbo, "How One Company is Providing Jobs for Those with Autism," *Forbes*, September 8, 2020, https://www.forbes.com/sites/jennifer palumbo/2020/09/08/provide-jobs-for-those-with-autism/?sh =3f20489810cf.
5. Tom D'Eri, e-mail to author, October 19, 2020.
6. Julie Fox, "A Neurodiverse Workforce," *MIT Technology Review*, October 24, 2019.
7. Ultranauts, "Onshore Quality Engineering Services," New York, September 2020.
8. Morgan Simon, "Thriving during COVID: Lessons from a team that is 75% autistic, 100% remote and 2X less lonely," *Forbes*, March 30, 2020. Anandan explains, "Today's businesses operate in unfathomably complex ecosystems, and while big data, machine learning and AI have tremendous potential to drive value across the enterprise, the very complexity of those technologies create a multitude of hidden risks and costs . . . That's what we do at Ultranauts, and the cognitive diversity of our team allows us to do this better than others and deliver superior value for our customers."
9. Alison Reynolds and David Lewis, "Teams Solve Problems Faster When They're More Cognitively Diverse," *Harvard Business Review*, March 30, 2017.
10. Byran Dai, interview with author, December 14, 2020.
11. Ibid.
12. Chet Hurwitz and Sara Barron, interview with author, September 29, 2020.
13. Tom D'Eri, e-mail to author, October 19, 2020.
14. In early 2018, REDF identified 162 "employment" social enterprises around the nation, within and outside of the REDF network.
15. Chapter 14 of *The Autism Job Club* also discussed the social enterprise movement as of 2014. This discussion recaps some of the observations in 2014, and updates the social enterprise movement to 2020.
16. REDF, "Social Enterprise Organizations Listening Session," March, 2018, www.redf.org.

17. National Council on Disability, "A Cursory Look at the AbilityOne Program," Washington, DC, National Council on Disability, 2019, https://ncd.gov/publications/2019/cursory-look-abilityone.
18. National Council on Disability, "Policies from the Past in a Modern Era: The Unintended Consequences of the AbilityOne Program & Section 14c," Washington, DC, October 2020.
19. Beyond federal contracting are the opportunities with state and local government contracting. Javits and REDF have succeeded in expanding contracting opportunities for social enterprises with local governments in Los Angeles County and Cook County, Illinois, and setting preference points for social enterprises in twelve counties in California.
20. REDF, "2021 National Policy Recommendations," San Francisco, REDF, 2020, https://redf.org/wp-content/uploads/REDF-2021-National-Policy-Recommendations.pdf.

11

EMPLOYMENT FOR THE MORE SEVERELY IMPACTED IN THE AUTISM COMMUNITY

For the more severely impacted adults with autism, the Act will champion mainstream employment placements. But it will also look beyond mainstream employment to other workplace structures, with realistic financial supports.

Most of the autism employment initiatives in recent years have focused on adults with "mild/moderate" autism. The Act will bring attention to adults more severely impacted. It will start with mainstream employment placements for these adults. But it will look beyond such placements, when they are not realistic or appropriate.

The alternatives need not be limited to mainstream employment (also known as competitive integrated employment) or no employment. Three other strategies have shown promise: (i) autism focused businesses that serve the most severely impacted, (ii) a restructuring of the congregate workshops, and (iii) forms of public service employment.

In chapter 13, Dr. Vismara presents a personal account of the job search for his son Mark, twenty-seven, who is one of these adults more severely impacted. Here let's look more broadly at current and possible strategies.

Part I: Current Employment Services for the More Severely Impacted

A government-funded infrastructure of employment services exists in all states, to serve adults with significant physical and developmental disabilities—a growing population due mainly to the increase in autism cases. In California, for example, the state disability department, the Department of Developmental Services (DDS), provided services to 256,216 individuals in 2014. Within five years that number had climbed to 333,010, and the number is projected to over 360,000 adults in 2021.[1]

The rise in autism diagnoses has been the main driver of caseloads. An estimated 70 percent of new cases are individuals with autism. Up through the early 1980s, autism cases constituted less than 5 percent of the DDS population. Today, one in three DDS clients is an individual with autism.

Employment is set out as a main goal for adults in the DDS system, for those with autism and those with other diagnoses. Toward this goal, the system provides a range of job assessment, job placement/job retention services, and an Independent Program Plan (IPP) developed for each adult.[2]

Even with these employment services, the paid employment rate for all DDS adults in 2020 was in the range of 16 percent. For adults with autism, the rate of paid employment was even lower, ranging from 14 percent in the Sacramento region, to 9 percent in the San Diego region.[3]

The preferred employment for DDS adults is "community integrated employment," defined as employment in mainstream settings that is paid at least minimum wage. Given the low levels of competitive employment achieved so far, DDS and other state disability departments are testing system adjustments, including incentive payments to providers,[4] alternative forms of job coaching, and better coordination of disability employment services among state departments.[5]

Autism advocates in California are in agreement with DDS that competitive employment is the preferred approach. But those advocates most connected to the severely impacted do not believe that system adjustments will result in significant employment gains. They regard competitive employment for many adults severely impacted as unrealistic ("a fantasy" in the words of one advocate), and urge looking to other venues.

Part II: Beyond Competitive Integrated Employment

Jill Escher is the president of the National Council on Severe Autism, dedicated to "solutions for the surging population of individuals, families and caregivers affected by severe forms of autism and related disorders."[6] She has a severely impacted son, and has closely followed the employment programs for the severely impacted in California.

"Many adults with severe disabilities will be incapable of competitive integrated employment, understood as employment in mainstream settings," Escher emphasizes. "It is fruitless and misleading to pretend otherwise. The private sector and even most nonprofits are not equipped to handle adults with severe conditions. We need to stop pretending that making competitive integrated employment work is finding the right job coach, or wage subsidy, or trained supervisor."[7]

Instead, Escher advises, let's look at developing alternative workplaces, with proper supervision and support, ones with realistic financial backing. Even these will not be a fit for a good number of adults with serious behavioral challenges. Any employment is not realistic for them, at least for now. But the alternative work strategies will offer options for some.

What are these alternative work strategies? Three stand out that could provide the needed supports:

- Autism-focused businesses that serve the most severely impacted.
- The restructuring of congregate workshops and some of the current 14c settings.
- New forms of Public Service Employment.

The autism-focused businesses serving the most severely impacted: As we saw in the previous chapter, the existing autism-focused businesses hire a range of workers in skills and behavior. A small but growing set of the autism-focused businesses have made hiring the more severely impacted their mission. Extraordinary Ventures New York (EVNY) is such a business. EVNY was founded by Andrew and Melanie Schaffran, parents of a son, Brett, with autism. They closely studied the established Extraordinary Ventures North Carolina program, operating businesses in North Carolina for the more severely impacted, and in 2015 started EVNY to serve adults in Westchester County, New York. At the time, Andrew was a partner at the global law firm of Morgan Lewis. In 2019 he retired to work full-time on EVNY.

EVNY has three businesses currently in operation. EVNY Gifts produces packaged candles and custom bracelets, and sells these at farmers' markets, local crafts fairs, and private affairs. EVNY office service provides document shredding for local businesses and document digitizing. EVNY laundry provides commercial laundry services. They all are located at a Mt. Kisco site, with the workers shifting at times across the businesses.

Prior to the pandemic, EVNY employed eighteen to twenty adults—adults who were not finding roles in competitive employment. Most of these workers were able to work only four to six hours per week, due to the limited number of orders. But they and their families valued the opportunity to get out of their houses, and hoped for additional hours, if possible.

Though EVNY will never be a large-scale employer of the severely impacted, it can provide an employment safe haven for some. Such a haven can also be provided by other similar businesses. But only with a different business model that does not rely entirely on market viability. EVNY has been able to operate mainly due to the commitment of the Schaffrans and with support from other financial donors. Its long term survival and growth and growth of similar businesses will not occur without some new form of wage subsidies for the workforce.

Restructuring, but continuing, the congregate workshops: So too some form of wage subsidy for the workforce will be needed for the rebuilding of the network of congregate workshops, aimed at the more severely impacted.

The congregate workshop system has been under attack, nationally and in individual states, and shrinking over the past decade. Escher observes that these workshops have provided employment for the more severely impacted who do not have other options: "I was speaking recently with someone in Washington, DC who is fighting to end the congregate workshops. For most adults and families in our National Council on Severe Autism the closing of the workshops is not a choice between a congregate workshop and mainstream employment, it is between a congregate workshop and no job."[8]

Pride Industries has been one of the nation's largest congregate workshops, with a headquarters facility in Roseville, outside of Sacramento, and four other facilities in the region. Ten years ago Pride Industries employed nearly 1300 adults in its congregate facilities. Today, this number is down to 650 adults. The reduction has not been due to decreased business orders. Rather, it is linked to the reduced federal and state government supports for congregate facilities, and movement to eliminate these facilities.

This movement to eliminate congregate facilities finds expression in the recent report by the National Council on Disability, a leading nationwide disability council. The report, "From the New Deal to the Real Deal: Joining the Industries of the Future," calls for a phasing out of the congregate workshops in favor of a full commitment to competitive integrated employment. The report declares:

> The time is now to modernize employment service systems to move from New Deal subminimum wages to 'real deal' jobs in the mainstream of the economy. For people with disabilities to experience full participation in the 21st century economy, they must be supported to be entrepreneurs, inventors and businesspeople of the future.[9]

Who wouldn't want to see this? But how realistic is it to speak of adults who may have little or no language as entrepreneurs, investors, and businesspeople of the future? And the adults and their families recognize this. Vic Wursten, the senior vice president at Pride, notes that as Pride Industries has been under pressure to eliminate its congregate workshop jobs, the workers and family members have rallied and reached out to state officials to save these jobs. For the workers and family members, these jobs are a place to go to everyday that provide life structure.

In January 2012, a class lawsuit was filed in Oregon on behalf of eight individuals with developmental disabilities. The lawsuit claimed that Oregon unnecessarily segregated adults with disabilities in congregate workshops. Under a settlement agreement reached in 2015, the state was required to take all efforts to move adults in congregate workshops into competitive integrated employment. An Independent Monitor was appointed to oversee the process.

The Independent Monitor's most recent report issued in March 2019 shows how difficult the process has been for competitive integrated employment. The number of persons in congregate workshops statewide stood at 2806 in March 2013. By March 2018, that number had shrunk dramatically to 664. The majority of persons no longer in congregate workshops had not found competitive employment. Even counting workers placed in competitive settings for more than a few hours a week, the Independent Monitor's report indicates the number to be no more than 780, and probably closer to 598.[10]

The goal should be not the dismantling of the congregate workshops, but a rebuilding of the system, paying minimum wage. A few congregate workshops, like Pride Industries, are able to pay minimum wage now. But many others cannot support these wages and survive as business entities. Like the autism-focused businesses serving the severely impacted, the next congregate system will require a way for congregate businesses to make up the gap to minimum wage.

The related "14c program" (section 14c of the federal Fair Labor Standards Act), by which businesses employ workers with "a physical or mental disability" in defined circumstances at below minimum wage, will require a more widespread restructuring. But it is also an approach (jobs with adequate supports in integrated as well as congregate settings) that, rather than be eliminated, should be reformed, with minimum wage as the goal.[11]

Several attempts have been made in recent years to eliminate the 14c program, citing documented abuses: workers at 14c companies paid less than other workers doing similar tasks (without differences in performance), executives at the 14c companies receiving salaries over $500,000 annually, and large companies utilizing 14c subminimum wages as a competitive advantage.[12] In 2019, the "Transformation to Competitive Employment Act" was introduced in the Congress to phase out the 14c program: to freeze the issuance of any new 14c certificates, gradually eliminate the existing 14c certificates, and require payment of minimum wage.[13] The Act did not pass, but officials in the Biden Administration have announced an intention to restart a process of eliminating 14c workplaces.

But eliminating these workplaces, similar to eliminating the congregate workshops, will leave many adults with severe disabilities nowhere to go. Escher makes this point in an impassioned posting on the National Council on Severe Autism website.[14] The 14c programs, she writes, are not just about the wages, they often offer multiple benefits unavailable in the competitive workplace, including close supervision, therapeutic care, ongoing coaching, and social and recreational activities. "There is nothing 'discriminatory,'" she adds, "about jobs that protect the severely disabled from being fired or from the vicissitudes of the free market."

Escher points to her son and daughter who are "nonverbal, cannot follow even simple directions without continual guidance and exhibit an array of disruptive behaviors. It is not just unlikely, it is impossible that they would ever be hired for competitive wage jobs." Her conclusion: retaining a non-competitive work option for the severely disabled does not negate expansion of competitive employment for those capable of it.

Reforming the current 14c program will mean addressing the ways noted above that the program has been misused. As minimum wage is the goal, reform will also require some form of wage subsidies, just as with the autism-focused businesses and congregate workshops. In all three of these settings, wage subsidies will be a more viable and cost-effective approach than trying to take the competitive employment route as the sole route.

New forms of public service employment, targeting those severely impacted: Subsidized public sector job creation is the third of the three categories of alternative work strategies for fuller employment of those severely impacted. Such public sector job creation is now being done on a very small scale on projects across the nation in park and open space maintenance and cleaning, municipal landscaping, assistance in long term care facilities, and museum support.

Janet Lawson, the long-time director of Autistry Studios in San Rafael, California, a non-profit serving adults with autism, has partnered with the National Park Service on subsidized public service employment projects including trail and facility maintenance, trimming bushes/trees, and serving visitors in concession stands. She explains:

The Park Rangers report that the Autistry crews have been a great support and help at the parks. The Autistry crews have learned to identify the various invasive species present in the parks and have helped the Rangers both in maintaining the aesthetic landscaping of the parks as well as managing the balance of native plant life there.[15]

She has a similar partnership with the Western Railway Museum, providing subsidized positions for her adults with autism in scanning and archiving historical photographs, assisting in restoration projects, and working with Museum staff in specialty exhibits.

To what extent public service employment jobs can be developed—and whether they will be realistic for most adults among the more severely impacted—remains to be seen. Public service employment will not be a fit for all, just as the other two workplaces will not be a fit. But like these other two alternative workplaces, public service employment, established as enterprise units outside of traditional government settings, can often accommodate the supervision and supports needed.

***

COMPETITIVE INTEGRATED EMPLOYMENT should be the primary goal for adults served by the state disability departments. But the goal will not be realistic for all, and the Act will want to rebuild, not shun, alternative work settings

NOTES

1. To be eligible for DDS services, an individual must have a disability that begins before their eighteenth birthday, is expected to continue indefinitely, and presents a "substantial disability" as defined in the state's Welfare & Institutions Code. The Code sets out that a "substantial disability" includes, among others, persons with "intellectual disability, cerebral palsy, epilepsy

and autism." Eligibility is established through diagnosis and assessment performed by the Regional Centers.

2. California Department of Developmental Services, "California Competitive Integrated Employment (CIE) Blueprint," Sacramento, California, 2017, Retrieved September 2020, https://www.dor.ca.gov/Home/CieBlueprint forChange.

3. The employment services, as other services for DDS clients, are administered by the twenty-one Regional Centers in the state. The budget for DDS has climbed rapidly with the caseloads and was $8.2 billion in 2019. For the 2021–2022 year, it is projected to be 10.5 billion.

4. Ohio Department of Developmental Disabilities, "Funding System Re-Design for Ohio's Employment First Initiative," Columbus, Ohio, 2014. https://ohioemploymentfirst.org/up_doc/Ohio_DODD_Report_1_Funding_System_Re-Design.pdf

5. California Department of Developmental Services, "California Competitive Integrated Employment (CIE) Blueprint." Sacramento, California, 2017.

6. National Council on Severe Autism, accessed January 24, 2020, https://www.ncsautism.org/.

7. Jill Escher, interview with author, October 15, 2020.

8. Jill Escher, Interview with author, October 15, 2020.

9. National Council on Disability, "From the New Deal to the Real Deal," Washington, DC, October 2018. https://ncd.gov/publications/2018/new-deal-real-deal

10. Cathy Ficker Terrill, "Land v. Brown: 2018 Report to the Court," March 29, 2019, https://www.oregon.gov/dhs/EMPLOYMENT/EMPLOYMENT-FIRST/Documents/Lane-IndependentReviewer-Report-2018.pdf, retrieved December 2020.

11. 14c employers must obtain a certificate from the US Department of Labor that any workers paid below minimum wage would not be employed if they were required to be paid minimum wage. The justification is that without this option, these workers would not be employed at all.

12. Hillel Aron, "Lawsuit Takes Aim at Sheltered Workshops Where Disabled Workers Make Far Less Than Minimum Wage," Fair Warning, www.fairwarning.org, September 18, 2019. https://www.fairwarning.org/2019/09/hundreds-of-thousands-of-disabled-workers-still-make-less-than-minimum-wage/

13. S.260, "Transformation to Competitive Employment Act," introduced in the 116th Congress on January 29, 2019.

14. Jill Escher, "Biden's Opening Disability Policy Gambit Would Eliminate Crucial Programs for the Severely Disabled," National Council on Severe Autism, January 26, 2021, https://www.ncsautism.org/blog//biden-would-eliminate-jobs-for-severely-disabled.
15. Janet Lawson, e-mail to author, August 20, 2020.

12

"FALLING OFF THE CLIFF" AND TRANSITION

Young adults with autism may feel like they are "falling off the cliff" when they turn eighteen, and the structured K-12 services end. In fact, the transition resources available are considerable, varied, and growing.

"Falling off the cliff" is the term often used by worried parents and family members when young adults with autism and other developmental differences turn eighteen. For most of these youth, the wide range of educational and behavioral services provided by their local school districts ends abruptly. The numbers of these youth are growing rapidly: just among youth with a diagnosis of autism, 750,000–1,000,000 are projected to turn eighteen over the next decade.

In fact, the resources available for transition, often free of cost, are considerable and growing every day. Young adults with autism and their support teams need to understand and pursue these resources. The autism employment system is not lacking for options, though they often require persistence in accessing them.

Chief among these are the following three categories of resources: (i) pre-employment and work experience programs for youth who are having difficulty "getting launched," (ii) university-based programs aimed at youth with autism and career technical education programs, and (iii) unconventional approaches, based on ideas of craft and "back to the land."

Entry Points for Transition Services and Support Networks

The entry point for transitional services often will be through one of the hundreds of community agencies providing services to adults with developmental differences.

JEVS Human Services is one of the best-known of these community agencies, serving youth and adults in the Philadelphia area. JEVS customizes transitional services, with emphasis on work placements and supports, and connection to job certifications. At the end of this chapter are notes from JEVS counselors on the job searches of four youth with developmental differences. These notes illustrate the process of customization, work experience and additional schooling that will often be part of the transition process.

It cannot be emphasized enough that family members and support networks should bring whatever time, skills, and contacts they can to the transition process. It can be a confusing process for anyone to navigate on their own, and customization of services is a key to effectiveness.

"My son Sam, a young man with autism, is twenty, and is doing an internship our family helped develop with Sam with Pleasantville Community Television (PCTV), the community access station in Westchester County, New York," explains Andrea Conte. "We knew we couldn't rely on the disability service system alone for transition, and needed to get involved ourselves. It wasn't easy. We searched through many potential businesses connected to Sam's interest in video editing, before we secured PCTV."[1]

Sam's job is to edit video, integrating different angles with the dialogue and other visuals. "We didn't know beforehand, but it has turned out that Sam is very good at focusing on his editing," Conte says. "The station manager is pleased with Sam's product and told us that Sam has taken his passion for media into the studio."

A long road remains for Sam to find steady work in the highly competitive video editing field. But the internship/work experience that he and his family developed is a first transitional step.

Transition Programs Tailored to Youth without Clear Direction
The term "failure to launch" has emerged in the past decade to describe youth of all kinds who are out of high school but have not been able to move forward in terms of education/employment and independent living. It has been applied particularly to young adults with autism who are not engaged in purposeful activity.

"I hear from parents of their children who spend their time on video games, Netflix, and social media. Their children may have tried one or two things, without success, and then decided 'what's the point,'" Dr. Bryna Siegel, head of the Autism Center of Northern California, observes. "These young people need to be engaged, get out of their houses, perhaps start small in education or work experience, to get one or two successes under their belt."[2]

Different Brains in South Florida is one of several entities nationwide that has launched transition programs, focused on these youth. These programs start with getting youth out of the house and into activities. Debbi Siegel, the executive director of Different Brains, notes: "We too hear from parents, whose children with autism, who are over eighteen, can't seem to venture from their rooms. They are stuck."[3]

"In response we started a transitional 'Mentorship Program' four years ago, to get the youth unstuck, by bringing them into internships at Different Brains," Siegel continues. "We have a variety of internships: video editing and social media linked to the autism video series we produce, research linked to our blogs on autism and grant writing, administration. The actual skills are not as important as getting the youth to overcome their anxieties about even trying."

Different Brains has surrounded the internships with collective activities: a toastmasters club in which the interns practice public speaking skills, bimonthly meetings of the full group, in which the interns discuss their progress, and, at least prior to the pandemic, planned social activities.

"We've been so pleased with the results, in these four years," Siegel says. "Young people, emerging from their shells, taking the next step to community college and even university settings, or vocational programs. We started with five or six interns in the first years, and are now up to fourteen."

University and Vocational Outreach to Youth with Developmental Differences

The "failure to launch" programs connect youth with colleges, but also colleges and universities have expanded their own outreach to youth with autism, not only in enrollment but adding social and academic supports. The College Link Program at Cal State University East Bay is one of the longer running programs.

For each student the Program develops a "University Education Plan," with similar intent to the high school Individualized Education Plan (IEP), setting goals and benchmarks. The services include extra tutors, academic coaching, weekly social activities, and a social skills group. The services are a mix of for-play and free of cost. Most other college programs also offer a basic level of free support services, with additional service levels for pay.

Nearly all of the 116 community colleges in California maintain the (anachronistically named) Disabled Student Programs and Services (DSPS) offices that provide services free of charge. At the community colleges, paid work experience is a priority for and available to most students with developmental differences.

One of the newest college developments: colleges are adding credential/certificate programs to serve students with autism and other developmental differences who are more severely impacted. The University of California, Davis, recently announced its Supported Education to Elevate Diversity (SEED) initiative, a four-year residential program to start with twelve students in Fall 2021. Students will attend UC Davis classes, be paired with peer mentors, work experience, and tutors. The expectation is not the BA degree, but some form of "meaningful credential" that the UC Davis MIND Institute is creating.

Post-secondary vocational programs at community colleges and private proprietary schools (nursing, cosmetology, long-term care nurse assistants, and child care) have been slower than universities to reach out to young adults with autism. Youth, though, are being connected to these programs, through the state vocational rehabilitation and disability departments, which in some cases will cover tuition costs. They are also being connected by the community agencies serving adults with developmental differences.

Transition through "Back to the Land" and Craft

Beyond the college, vocational, and pre-employment programs are less conventional transition programs that draw on older intellectual traditions regarding transition, emphasizing craft and the land. One of the most thoughtful of these is the Meristem program, near Sacramento, California.

The Meristem campus is set on thirteen bucolic acres outside of Sacramento: a series of pastel cottages spread among a working farm, woodworking and metal shops, a bakery, walking trails, and orchards. Its design and curriculum are based on the Ruskin Mill Trust, founded in England in 1987 to serve young adults with mental health and learning disabilities, rooted in the ideas of the nineteenth century art critic turned social advocate, John Ruskin.[4]

In the mid-1980s, the founders of the Ruskin Mill Trust discovered in Ruskin's ideas on land and craft what they believed to be a transition path for youth with disabilities. Over the past thirty years, the Trust has succeeded in building land-and-craft-based transition centers throughout England and Wales. Prominent Sacramento philanthropists Marc

Turtletaub and Maureen Curran-Turtletaub visited these centers and, inspired, established Meristem in the Sacramento suburb of Fair Oaks, with a first cohort of students in 2015.

The Meristem curriculum, a two to three year program, is a structured one, combining classes in farming, the crafts (metal, wood, baking, and the culinary arts) physical exercise, and movement. Accompanying the training, the Meristem students also work in the businesses that Meristem has established—Meristem Bakery, Meristem Herbal products, and Meristem Model Bed and Breakfast.

Meristem officials envision that some students will pursue careers in farming and the crafts. But the training is aimed mainly at other values: self-confidence, shedding of anxieties, self-advocacy, and social participation. More than technical skills, these are the values that might overcome the isolation and marginality common in the past to adults with autism and other disabilities.

Edmund Knighton, the Meristem president, has written on the relation of craft and autism. Through craft, young adults practice discipline and persistence, with an emphasis on results. Referring to one student, Ben, who had a withdrawn and remote demeanor prior to Meristem, Knighton explains, "Ben receives objective feedback from the materials he sculpts or hammers or weaves. When successful, the product has value for others and the world because it is functional. With practice, students discipline themselves to persist through boredom, conflict with themselves and with others, and fatigue. As they are supported by instructors and peers to work through these challenges, their work becomes not only more functional but also more aesthetic."

Beyond craft, the connection to the land and natural environment is meant to reduce anxieties, provide grounding, and sharpen the ability to see things whole. Knighton details this connection to the land and farming in the following terms: "Students experience the full cycle of organic/biodynamic plant life, from sprouting the pastel to planting and weeding and watering and harvesting it. Then they clean it and use it as an ingredient in our bakery or café to serve to the community. Experiencing the full cycle of a food substance that grows and then allows us to grow provides a deeply satisfying wholeness to our students, in contrast to so much in life that feels disconnected or in conflict. Lunch is a time where all staff and students sit down together and share a meal from the garden."[5]

Meristem has grown from a few students in 2015 to a cohort of forty-five, with a waiting list, and ideas of expanding to other locations in California. Students are becoming involved in the local Sacramento community, through taking classes at America River Community College and other local colleges. The Meristem businesses, especially the bakery, are venturing out to sell to the area residents—pushing students to practice sales and executive skills. This year Meristem is forming its own youth chapter of the Rotary Club.

Dr. Vismara is a former Meristem board member. While on the board, he would take time to meet with new Meristem students and follow their experiences, and writes of his findings: "Upon enrollment, many of Meristem's students manifested aloof and withdrawn behaviors. When I first met with members of the entering cohort, their anxiety, stress, and detachment was pervasive and truly palpable. During the in course of Meristem's program, virtually all of the students demonstrated a great sense of identity, purpose, and self-confidence."

***

PRACTITIONERS EMPHASIZE THAT in choosing among transitional resources, there is no "right" approach. What's important is that these resources be understood, and that individuals and families recognize that they do not have to "go it alone." Further, the transition process of finding a fit in the job market can take several false starts and failures. It can take multiple attempts and longer term perspective over years.

***

Transition Service Notes from Counselors at the JEVS Program in Philadelphia

Below are notes on a number of recent employment transitions of youth with developmental differences served by the JEVS program in Philadelphia. They indicate how long the process can take, as well as the customization.

#1-C.S.: One of our youngest members, twenty-two years old. Prior to coming to JEVS, he tried attending two different independent living college experience programs. Both programs are out of state. While in these programs, he experienced a lot of social anxiety and decided he needed to be closer to his family in the Philadelphia area.

Throughout his first year as part of JEVS, he had a part-time job as part of the maintenance team at a private school. He was very unhappy in this job, and often talked of his dream to work for SEPTA, the public transportation system in Philadelphia.

He is an expert on public transportation systems in Philadelphia as well as many other major metropolitan areas. He is particularly interested in trains and is extremely knowledgeable about the broader operation of public transit systems, as well as the mechanics of various types of trains. Since he was a teenager, he has attended the monthly SEPTA board meetings that are open to the public. He is well-known for his public comments and interest in improving the operations of public transportation systems. In the last week of June in 2016, he was offered a job by SEPTA as an undercover rider to assess various elements of customer satisfaction of both SEPTA bus and subway riders. This opportunity was a dream come true!

He continues to work for SEPTA and recently became a peer mentor to assist other young adults with disabilities to learn how to use public transportation.

#2-K: He has been part of the JEVS "Philadelphia Independence Network" (PIN) for nearly seven years. At the start of K's PIN journey he was very hesitant to work due to being nervous and having very little work experience. We began by helping K to find volunteer opportunities and supported him to volunteer. After a short time, K found volunteering to be too overwhelming and decided to stop volunteering. He made it clear that employment was not his most pressing priority.

K watched as many of his peers in the program got jobs. He genuinely celebrated their accomplishments and enthusiastically recognized their efforts. The PIN team periodically asked K if he was ready to begin considering employment. However, it never seemed to be the right moment. Time passed, and about a year ago K approached the PIN team to let us know he was ready to begin searching for paid employment. In October, K obtained his first job as a dishwasher at Anthony's Coal Fired Pizza. Since starting his job, K has gradually increased his responsibilities and hours to almost full-time!

#3-J: J has been a member of the PIN program since November 2013. During her tenure with PIN, J has experienced a lot of change and transition. She has struggled to find the right job as a result of limited work history. Despite many and varied changes, J has persevered and maintained hope as she has discovered more about her career interests and directions.

In the fall of 2018, J expressed interest in pursuing a career in the beauty industry as a professional makeup artist or cosmetologist. This interest was quite a shift from previous paths she identified. The Career Navigator urged J to take her time and fully explore this new direction. Together, they identified several local schools and educational opportunities—both formal and informal. J received support to visit and tour multiple schools. With the help of the Career Navigator, she set up times to shadow students in two different schools. Finally, J applied to a few schools and worked to access financial aid that would allow her to become a full-time student. As of January 2019, J enrolled as a full-time student at the Jean Madeline Aveda Institute and is working toward her certification in cosmetology. J is enthusiastic and very hopeful about her next steps!

#4-C: C joined PIN in October 2015. She moved to Narberth to live on her own for the first time. In order to move, she had to leave a job she loved in a New Jersey after-school program. Shortly after C moved, PIN staff helped her to find a job providing childcare at a local gym. She experienced great success in this position—the parents, children, and gym staff grew to love her! Eventually, C wanted more. She wanted to return to the structure of a preschool classroom and challenge herself to take on more of a teacher's assistant role. C searched for jobs and found an opportunity at a Montessori-based preschool. She applied and obtained a part-time position. C quickly expressed how much she loved being back in the preschool environment. Her new employer recognized her talents, but also was clear that without a CDA or Child Development Associate certificate she would not be able to progress in the school. C decided that she wanted to pursue the certificate. With the help of her parents, she found a school where she could take classes on the weekends and still maintain her job. For six months, she attended school on the weekends. During the week, the PIN Career Navigator helped her to complete assignments and prepare for the exam. C finished classes, and for several months studied for the upcoming exam, prepared for classroom observations, and helped her to gain confidence in her knowledge and skills. Each week she was supported to study and practice skills. Finally, in January 2019, C took the exam. She passed!! C is now a certified CDA. This accomplishment allows her to work independently with children and has afforded her additional pay, hours, and responsibilities. C is taking the next steps in her career!

NOTES

1. Andrea Conte, interview with author, October 27, 2020.
2. Bryna Siegel, interview with author, November 3, 2020.
3. Debbi Siegel, interview with author, November 5, 2020.
4. Though Ruskin (1819–1900) first achieved public prominence in the 1840s and 1850s with a series of art histories and criticisms, by 1860 he had turned from art criticism to trying to remake Victorian society. He railed against industrialization and its division of labor as the degradation of work, and called for a return to the land and the practical arts. Receiving a large inheritance upon the death of his father in 1864, he put his ideas into practice, funding through his Guild of St. George businesses that employed workers in hand-producing cloth goods, textiles, and fresh foods.
5. Edmund Knighton, email to author, January 8, 2020.

13

LESSONS LEARNED FROM MARK: A PERSONAL STORY BY DR. LOUIS VISMARA

As a physician I was privileged to practice interventional cardiology for almost three decades. During my medical training I was drawn to this particular specialty because it provided excellent tools to not only evaluate patients, but, more importantly, to quickly intervene in order to correct their problems with a high degree of success. The mindset of initially identifying a problem, evaluating it carefully, and trying to correct the problem as quickly as possible has become deeply ingrained in my professional and personal life. Recently, I have realized that unwittingly I've adopted this same approach since our son, Mark, was diagnosed at eighteen months of age with a severe form of Autism Spectrum Disorder (ASD).

After Mark's diagnosis, like so many other families, we were frustrated by the lack of funding and coordinated scientific research, so we worked with other advocates to establish premier academic centers such as the UC Davis MIND Institute. During the past twenty-some years, there have been remarkable breakthroughs in our understanding of the science and causes of autism. The early detection, evaluation, treatment, and medical insurance coverage for this disorder have markedly improved. Despite these noteworthy and inspiring advances, employment opportunities for people with autism remain woefully lacking. Arguably, transitional services, vocational training, and competitive integrated employment are significantly lacking (some would say virtually absent) for individuals such as our son who require intensive supports and accommodations.

During the past several years, my wife Wendy and I have focused on providing Mark with his own life that optimizes his potential for growth, independence, and self-satisfaction. A major emphasis of our endeavors has been related to finding jobs and employment for Mark. Even as I write the preceding sentence, part of my brain is saying, "Lou, shouldn't you be looking for jobs 'with Mark, and NOT for Mark?'" Nothing would give me greater joy and pleasure than if indeed that could be the case. Regretfully, Mark would not be a candidate to work at Microsoft or SAP. For reasons that hopefully will become evident, even working at an Amazon warehouse or Walgreens facility are well beyond his capacities and capabilities.

Vocational training and opportunities for sustained, competitive integrated employment are (in my opinion) virtually absent for individuals such as Mark, who require intensive support and accommodations. This problem is further intensified by recent federal and state rulings that many of the congregate settings and day programs are being phased out. Adhering to the old adage of "every crisis presents a golden opportunity," Wendy and I have been "beating the bushes and leaving no stone unturned" in finding jobs for Mark.

As a prelude for discussing our hopes and aspirations for Mark's future employment, I must provide an overview of the challenges and limitations that Mark seeks to overcome on a daily basis. The realization and acceptance of Mark's severe limitations have been a difficult personal journey. For many years, I struggled with the misguided belief that we could either "cure" Mark of his autism or provide enough therapy and/or support so that he could have "a normal life." A few years ago, a friend gently informed me that my hopes were as ill-founded as my trying to dunk a basketball (I'm 5'9" and can't jump). Furthermore, I've come to the realization that an honest and accurate assessment of Mark's capabilities and limitations is a key and crucial element to finding purposeful and meaningful activities in his life.

Mark, who is twenty-seven years old, is our only son and the youngest of four children. His three sisters are all neuro-typical, highly educated, and without any disabilities or special needs. Mark's gestation, delivery, and first year of life were all unremarkable. However, his subsequent lack of speech and language development resulted in the diagnosis of Autism Spectrum Disorder at the age of eighteen months. Prompt intensive early intervention, applied behavior analysis (ABA) therapy, resulted in some developmental improvements and a modicum of functional language, but early attempts at "mainstream" educational classrooms were unsuccessful.

Individuals such as Mark with severe autism present a dizzying and frequently overwhelming array of symptoms, problems, and conundrums. An issue that has been especially perplexing in our son's case is the potential for an extreme variability in his moods, behaviors, and actions. At times, Mark will be engaged, behaving appropriately, and seemingly in good spirits. Yet, his good mood can evaporate in seconds. Aggressive or self-injurious behaviors have previously appeared in a flash. Fortunately, during the past several years these physical outbursts have become extremely infrequent and are currently nonexistent. Nevertheless, there are still times when Mark will become inexplicably agitated. These episodes are frequently accompanied by brief shouts and verbal outbursts, which are symptoms that have raised the possibility of Tourette's syndrome.

Understandably, these highly variable, and at times uncontrollable, utterances and inappropriate behaviors pose severe complications to most, if not all, integrated workplace environments. However, we have found that these challenges, although at times extremely difficult, are not insurmountable. Let me underscore that these insights and recommendations are strictly anecdotal, based only on our family's personal experiences and must be tailored for each individual. Nevertheless, I would like to share some of the strategies and approaches that may be helpful in obtaining employment opportunities for autistic individuals who are overcoming significant behavioral-communication issues and require intensive supports.

Begin with the End in Mind

It is absolutely imperative to seek and identify employment opportunities that are consistent with each individual with autism's strengths and abilities. In our son's case, having a specific "check-list" or SWOT (Strength, Weakness, Opportunities, Threats) was helpful. Examples of Mark's "Strengths" include: strong and very well coordinated; enjoys being active; no physical limitations; does well in a structured and consistent environment; visual learner; and reasonable receptive language. His weaknesses include the following: essentially nonverbal; limited interests in social engagement; variable mood swings; occasional verbal outbursts; intermittent anxiety; and tendency to perseveration (repetition of a particular response). These (and other weaknesses) may lead to examples of the following "Threats," the most serious being that his disruptive behaviors could interfere with not only his productivity, but also have a major negative impact with his co-workers and his job environment. Examples of other potential "threats" include: communication difficulties, lack of spontaneity and flexibility, and problem-solving abilities. Which leads us to the issue of "opportunities," i.e. what type of job(s) could possibly lead to Mark's successful long-term employment. Based on multiple detailed discussions with Mark's behaviorists and support staff, Mark's support team proposed the following: that Mark's employment opportunities should ideally include as many as possible of the following possibilities:

Structured Environment

Mark, like so many other individuals with ASD, has always had difficulties coping with transitional situations and/or a changing environment. These challenges are especially heightened when exposed to new circumstances, and increased demands and during concurrent periods of increased stress, anxiety, or other emotional instability. Although these difficulties and challenges will be inevitably associated with any/all employment opportunities, in my opinion it is of paramount importance and absolutely crucial that we seek only those jobs that can be associated with a stable and highly structured work environment. In identifying a structured environment, I would consider the following factors:

1. Consistency: The tasks, activities, and job requirement are similar (if at all possible) on a daily or regular basis.
2. Predictable: That Mark will know ahead of time what jobs/activities are scheduled for that particular day or "timeframe." We have found that having a various visual schedule(s), timers, and other monitoring devices/prompts are all of utmost importance in having him understand and successfully cope with various employment activities.
3. Linear activities: Mark can become easily bored with pursuing the same type of work over prolonged periods of time. Therefore, we've tried to find occupations that enable him to establish a natural flow where various types of activities can be integrated in a natural and successful work environment. For example, prior to the COVID pandemic, Mark worked in the dining room of a large assisted living facility that served over a hundred seniors daily. His job required that he clear all of the tables, clean and vacuum the dining area, and prepare the tables and room for the evening meal. In essence he was able to change activities in a way that were logical, predictable, and clearly had a beginning and an end to each of the various tasks. Furthermore, this schedule

enabled him to change activities during his work period (ultimately two to three hours) that provided a significant degree of satisfaction and accomplishment.

Vocational Training

Regretfully, in my experience, vocational training was limited throughout Mark's education. Although Mark was enrolled in various excellent special education classes with highly dedicated teachers, all too often the academic programs and curriculum did not apply to getting a job in the real world. Furthermore, his experiences with several work experience programs (under the Workability II government program) also failed to impart any significant post-secondary job skills.

Therefore, we have sought employment opportunities whereupon vocational job skills can be:

1. Acquired initially outside of the workplace. For example, many of Mark's skills in learning how to work at the senior assisted living facility were initially acquired by having him practice the same identical chores at various home settings.

2. Vocational organizations/programs. We have been very fortunate that Mark has been employed at Pride Industries, which is the nation's largest employer of individuals with disabilities. We found that his work experience at Pride provided an invaluable experience in working around other individuals and being part of a productive goal-oriented team.

3. Employer accommodations: We were extremely blessed that Eskaton Senior Care & Services was willing to provide a trial period during which Mark could learn and acquire the necessary skills to work at their assisted living facility dining room. What was also incredibly heartwarming and uplifting was the manner in which the assisted living residents welcomed (and, in some cases, embraced) Mark and several other of his developmentally disabled coworkers. I am truly hopeful that post-COVID, Mark

will not only resume working at Eskaton, but that we may find other employment opportunities related to services and support for older adults.

Employment Support

I believe that many of the most important factors related to employment opportunities for individuals like Mark are dependent on activities that start long before job placement is contemplated. Our family's experiences include the following observations and conclusions:

1. Soft-skills training: Soft skills are non-technical skills that relate to how you work. They include how you interact with colleagues, how you solve problems, and how you manage your work. Soft skills are the skills that enable you to fit in at a workplace. They include your personality, attitude, flexibility, motivation, and manners. It's especially important to identify and address these issues for ASD individuals, such as Mark, who require intensive accommodations and support. For Mark, some examples of these soft skills included: being comfortable in a strange environment; adjusting to ambient background noises and other distractions; being around strangers; and acquiring anxiety-coping mechanisms other than verbal outbursts, to mention only a few. In summary, soft skills are extremely important but should be focused on strategies and outcomes that enable the autistic individual to feel comfortable, relax, and focus on the job at hand.

2. Job Coach: Mark is currently enrolled in California's Supported Living Services (SLS) Program. This program consists of a broad range of services to adults with developmental disabilities who live apart from their families and are supported by an array of staff and services to secure the maximum possible level of personal independence. We are blessed to have an amazing group of individuals who have not only supported him at him home and in the community but have also performed admirably and have

been incredibly effective as his job coaches in various endeavors. Their high degree of success has been directly linked to the following:

a. *Knowing and communicating with Mark*. They all have an incredible awareness of Mark's moods, anxieties, and stress levels such that they are able to either redirect him in a positive or productive manner, and/or provide prompt interventions to deescalate any untoward situation before it arises.

b. *A trusting relationship*. It is equally important that Mark knows and trusts the staff. Therefore, his levels of anxiety and stress during the initial period(s) of employment accommodation are naturally going to be much lower and amenable to effective vocational training.

c. *Incremental approach*. Since the staff are part of Mark's regular daily activities and routines, his staff can adjust his pre-employment vocational training in a flexible and incremental manner. With this approach, Mark's time on the job can be gradually increased without disrupting the rest of his other activities and routines.

d. *Promoting independence*. Since Mark's staff is with him during eight-hour shifts, it's much easier for them to gradually reduce their role as job coach and encourage Mark's independence—while being on standby should Mark encounter any unexpected problems.

Engagement and Assessment

When we first met with disability employment specialists, invariably they asked, "What does Mark like to do and what kind of jobs or activities is he interested in doing?" Unfortunately, our persistent (and only) response that he loves to watch TV, especially train videos, was not helpful and often led to abbreviated interviews.

Since Mark has extremely limited inherent interests, we have taken a different approach. Specifically, we first find a job situation that is highly structured, consistent, and provides the appropriate vocational training and support. Subsequently we then implement a gradual and incremental approach to each job and/or activity. Multiple steps, usually concurrent, are involved. Factors that we have found helpful include the following:

1. Time limits: Starting with a shorter period of time for each activity tends to avoid anxiety, frustrations, and behaviors and instead promotes a feeling of accomplishment. Often having a timer or other form(s) of visual reference may also be helpful. These prompts are also useful in gradually increasing the duration for the job in question.

2. Reward and Compensation: Motivation to work is invariably related to "getting something out of it." Therefore, we have always tried to link new challenges for Mark with some sort of reward or activity that he enjoys and associates with the task. Although we try to avoid food-related rewards as much as possible, an occasional trip to the ice cream store may be desirable. Other rewards have included small stipends that enable him to purchase favorite DVDs; trips to our favorite balloon store; visits to the Railroad Museum; or simply downtime that enable him to watch his favorite TV program or video. However, it's important that we use a visual schedule or other forms of communication such that Mark associates the "reward" with and as the direct consequence of "doing and completing his job."

3. Backward Chaining: When teaching life skills to individuals with special needs, this term refers to breaking down the steps of a task and teaching them in reverse order. For example, setting a dinner table at Eskaton began with our job coach doing all of the initial work (i.e. getting all of the utensils, placing the tablecloth, etc.) and then having Mark complete the setting by just placing all of the dishes in their appropriate places. After mastering that task, Mark was then required to place the glassware, then the

silverware, and so on until he could do everything by himself. In other words, during the vocational training process, the job coach does less and less while Mark did more and more, and always ended with him performing the final step. We have found that this is an important technique that is applicable to teaching a variety of jobs and other complex behaviors.

Specific Jobs and Employment Opportunities

1. Services for Older Adults: As I said previously, prior to the onset of the COVID pandemic, Mark had been working for several years at an Eskaton assisted facility dining area, which served about 110 residents daily. His job consisted of clearing the cafeteria area after lunch; vacuuming and thoroughly cleaning the area; and preparing the dining room for the evening meal. Mark enjoyed and was quite capable in this endeavor, since it provided a quiet, consistent, repetitive, and highly structured environment. We anticipate that he will resume this activity after the pandemic crisis has been resolved.

   Mark's employment at Eskaton was also noteworthy due to the rapport and empathy that was evident between Mark and the residents. Although essentially nonverbal, Mark is quite attuned and sensitive to ambiances and general vibes. Being in a welcoming and warm environment was an important factor in Mark's successful employment. We've noticed a similar type of rapport in other facilities and circumstances between seniors and adults with autism. In some situations, older adults just enjoyed being in the same room and "hanging out" with some of the employees with autism. Therefore, we're hopeful that post-COVID, Mark may expand his employment at Eskaton to other activities such as housekeeping, transportation, culinary, and other support services.

2. Vending Machines: The "microenterprise concept" is another opportunity that merits consideration. Several autistic individuals

have been successful in starting their own food trucks, bakeries, coffee shops, delicatessens, or other independent endeavors. Since the complexities of running a business exceed Mark's potential and capabilities, we've just started another project: Mark's vending machine business. Specifically, we've purchased two vending machines that are located in the lobby of a large (seventy thousand square foot) commercial office building.

This venture has required Mark (with staff support) to do the following on a weekly basis: 1) Take inventory of both machines; 2) Purchase bulk quantities of thirty to forty different types of products; and 3) Restock both machines. These activities have resulted in the following outcomes and benefits: 1) Mark is much better at learning to count and understand numeric concepts; 2) He is more comfortable in large shopping (i.e. "big-box") environments; 3) He has improved organizational skills; and 4) The venture is economically viable and we are currently in the process placing vending machines in several other sites.

3. Dog-Walking Service: For the past several years Mark and his staff have been providing dog-walking services for three families, all of whom live in Mark's neighborhood. These activities, which are scheduled on a regular and consistent basis, average in total about six hours per week. We have found that Mark not only enjoys the regular exercise, but that consistent physical activity has a pronounced calming effect that significantly reduces his levels of anxiety and stress. In view of his active and consistent appetite, his regular walking schedule also keeps him fit and trim.

Furthermore, Mark's dog-walking service has provided a nice conduit and potential for social interactions. Not only does he interact with the dog-owners families, but his consistent jaunts throughout his community have enabled him, and his staff, to meet and interact with many of his neighbors and even make some friends. Learning to bake is another unanticipated benefit of this activity. Since we recently realized that Mark enjoys feeding snacks to the animals, my wife Wendy has been teaching Mark to bake his own dog biscuits. This process has also been helpful in promoting Mark's organizational skills, learning to initiate and complete sequential tasks, and, most importantly, the satisfaction of a personal accomplishment: i.e. feeding his biscuits to the dogs.

I was told many years ago that as we go through life, all of us need, *"A job, a home, and a friend."* For individuals with autism such as Mark, a job is especially important since it can serve as a conduit to friendships, social interactions, and as the gateway to a greater sense of freedom, independence, and self-worth. I am hopeful that our family's efforts in exploring and promoting our son's employment opportunities will not only improve the quality of Mark's life, but may also provide a modicum of benefit to other families and individuals who are overcoming similar challenges.

14

COMORBIDITIES AND MENTAL HEALTH CONDITIONS

In this chapter, Dr. Vismara discusses comorbidities and mental health issues related to autism employment.

Comorbidities, mental health conditions concomitant or concurrent with autism, can be major barriers to successful employment outcomes. As we have seen in our own families, and with many other adults with Autism Spectrum Disorder (ASD), these conditions are not easily addressed. They are often deep rooted and neurologically based.

We are learning more every day about the neurology of autism and about strategies for addressing these conditions and/or managing them for jobs and independent living. These strategies are not effective in all cases; and in most cases, they will take time and multiple dead ends and unsuccessful efforts before any success. But medical professionals are seeing evidence of effectiveness.

Chief among the comorbidities linked to ASD are the following four: Obsessive-compulsive disorder (OCD), Attention Deficit

Hyperactivity Disorder (ADHD), Anxiety Disorder, and Major Depressive Disorder.

Below, we'll briefly discuss these comorbidities, how they can undermine employment, and the approaches for managing them.

Part I: Comorbidities Linked to Autism and Their Neurobiology

Recent advances in our understanding of neurobiology and brain function indicate that various mental health and behavioral disorders are associated with comparable anomalies and irregularities. For example, recent genome research has indicated that specific parts of the human genome are similar, have a common sequence, and overlap among various behavioral disorders.

Among the major studies in recent years is the one by the Psychiatric Genomics Consortium, a collaboration of researchers in nineteen countries and led by Harvard professor Dr. Jordan Smoller, which examined the genetic coding of more than thirty-three thousand psychiatric patients and compared them to nearly twenty-eight individuals without mental illness.[1] All parts of the human genetic codes were evaluated in both groups.

The results indicated that five behavioral disorders, including ASD, ADHD, and major depressive disorder all shared identical risks in the same four segments of the human genetic code. The researchers noted that although this study does not explain the cause of these disorders (hundreds and perhaps thousands of genetic abnormalities have been implicated in various behavioral disorders) the results suggest that these five disorders are more like a continuum of dysfunction than five separate and discrete conditions. The conclusions of this report also make sense from a clinical perspective, since many individuals with behavioral disorders not only have overlapping symptoms (i.e. schizophrenia may manifest social withdrawal associated with ASD) but also have co-existing psychiatric conditions.

Other recent studies indicate that almost 75 percent of individuals with ASD would also meet criteria for at least one other mental health disorder as classified by the DSM-IV. There is also evidence that the incidence of psychiatric comorbidities with ASD may be significantly greater than are noted with other types of intellectual or developmental disabilities. One report noted that among a cohort of individuals with ASD, 17 percent of the sample group had two additional mental/behavioral health disorders and another 24 percent exhibited three or more of these disorders.[2] Regretfully these concomitant psychiatric disorders are either frequently overlooked or considered to be an inherent aspect of the underlying ASD disorder.

Although the current healthcare system, which includes provider networks, support services, and safety-net organizations, has established distinct categorical differences between autism and behavioral/mental health diseases, there are a number of overlapping issues among these disorders. Future behavioral health initiatives may benefit from a functional approach that takes into account the co-existing aspects of ASD and mental health disorders.

Part II: Four of the Main Comorbidities and Treatment Options

Obsessive–compulsive disorder (OCD) is a specific type of anxiety disorder that is characterized by intrusive thoughts that result in recurring and repetitive cycles of thoughts and behaviors. Consequently, individuals with OCD, in a compensatory effort to reduce their apprehension and fears, engage in ritualistic behaviors and perseverative behaviors and compulsive routines. Symptoms of OCD may include extreme hoarding, excessive washing and cleaning, fear of behaving in a socially unacceptable manner, need for constant reassurance, demand for exactness, repeating specific words or phrases, repeatedly checking things, and needing to perform tasks a certain number of times. Although the cause of OCD is undetermined, researchers have noted a link between low levels of serotonin, an important brain neurotransmitter, and the development of OCD. Roughly one third to one half of adults with OCD report a childhood onset of the disorder.

A concurrent psychiatric diagnosis of OCD has been reported to vary between 8 percent to more than 33 percent of individuals with ASD. A meta-analysis study by van Steensel and colleagues that evaluated anxiety-related conditions presented concurrent to autism reported that 17 percent of people with an autism spectrum condition also presented with a verifiable DSM-IV diagnosis of OCD.[3] However, some level of perseverative and/or compulsive behavior has been reported in over 85 percent of individuals with ASD. Most frequently children with ASD demonstrate ritualistic manners that related to specific individuals, perseverative questions, or continuously repeating the same statement. Nearly half of the children with concurrent ASD and OCD manifested compulsions that involved highly structured actions that involved other individuals having to do things in a certain way.

In individuals with ASD, anxiety often develops because of the unpredictability, and it is reduced when an individual engages in repetitive behaviors. Obsessions and compulsions have been reported, with ASD, to function as a way of coping when the environment is unpredictable and as a means of helping to control the unpredictability. Thus, whereas individuals with OCD are frequently anxious or disturbed as a consequence of their obsessive compulsions, individuals with ASD are usually either not bothered or are actually comforted by their repetitive thoughts and behaviors.

Although OCD is a serious condition, which may be associated with high levels of disability, there are a number of potential treatments that may significantly improve individuals' ability to function and greatly improve their quality of life. Long-term studies suggest that 32–70 percent of people with OCD experience symptom remission, which suggests that recovery is a realistic, achievable goal for some people with the condition.[4] However, as in the case of essentially all other autism-related mental health comorbidities, the following observations have been noted:

1. Therapy must be highly individualized.
2. Therapy is often incremental and may require frequent adjustments over a prolonged period of time.
3. Symptoms may frequently vary, thereby making it difficult to evaluate the efficacy of the treatment(s).
4. Therapy frequently involves a combination of medication(s) and behavioral/psychological interventions.
5. Lack of outcome measures; regretfully there are no blood tests, surveys, or other forms of evaluation that will predict the likelihood of successful treatment.

Despite these limitations and challenges, a number of medications may be helpful in the treatment of OCD. Specifically, a class of drugs called selective serotonin reuptake inhibitors (SSRIs) are now approved by the Food and Drug Administration (FDA) for the treatment of this disorder. Although also frequently prescribed as antidepressants, in OCD they appear to reduce anxiety and improve neural pathways by enhancing the availability of serotonin, a substance crucial to normal brain function.

A combination of several medications that have different mechanisms of actions may also be helpful. Physicians are now exploring whether treatment of OCD with a combination of medications may be helpful. Since problems with dopamine (another neurotransmitter) are also implicated in OCD, medications such as Risperdal (risperidone), Zyprexa (olanzapine), or Seroquel (quetiapine) are also being evaluated for the treatment of OCD.

It's not unusual to try several drugs before finding one that works well. Furthermore, individuals with autism may be highly sensitive to these medications; a fact that I've observed to be overlooked by very competent physicians. I can't overemphasize the importance of effectively controlling symptoms at the lowest possible dosage.

In view of the highly variable response to medications, it's important that individuals, and their "circle of support," have a clear understanding and specific action plan with regard to the following:

1. Potential adverse reactions and side effects.
2. Potential onset of action(s), which may take weeks or months.
3. Potential interactions with other medications and substances.
4. Potential suicide risk. Although most antidepressants are generally safe, the FDA requires that all antidepressants carry the strictest warnings for an increase in suicidal thoughts or behavior when taking antidepressants, especially in the first few weeks after starting or when the dose is changed.
5. Stopping or missing medications, which can result in significant adverse reactions and/or a relapse of severe OCD symptoms.

Psychological therapy and counseling may also be effective in reducing the frequency and intensity of OCD symptoms. Cognitive-behavioral therapy (CBT), which focuses on moods and thoughts as well as targeting specific actions and behaviors, may enable individuals with OCD to develop more constructive behavioral responses to challenging or stressful situations. CBT may also include Acceptance & Commitment Therapy (ACT), which seeks to accept unpleasant situations, not overreact, and to set meaningful personal goals. Another form of therapy, known as Exposure and Response Prevention (ERP), gradually exposes OCD individuals to stressful situations, activities, or behaviors while providing support and coping mechanisms that can mitigate the phobia-OCD cycle. Although all forms of counseling should always be considered, individuals with ASD may present unique challenges that include: 1) Limited self-awareness by some individuals with autism; 2) Limited receptive and expressive language; 3) Impaired intellectual function; and 4) Limited number of psychiatrists or therapists with ASD expertise.

It has been estimated that between 25 and 40 percent of OCD individuals fail to adequately respond to a combination of medication and/or psychotherapy. Additional interventions include some common-sense approaches such as a healthy diet, adequate sleep, and various relaxation techniques. There is preliminary evidence that exercise can also reduce the symptoms of OCD. More radical approaches, which are usually reserved for severe and debilitating cases of OCD, have included electroconvulsive therapy (ECT); deep brain stimulation; and even neurosurgical procedures that target specific areas of the brain.

More recently, Transcranial Magnetic Stimulation (TMS) has received considerable attention as a possible alternative treatment to reduce OCD symptoms. This noninvasive intervention has been shown to alter neural pathways by causing a focused magnetic field in the brain. TMS is generally considered as safe and adverse reactions, such as fainting seizures or discomfort, are rare. TMS has shown therapeutic potential in the central nervous system with a wide variety of disease states in neurology and mental health. However, research is still evolving and the evidence is currently inconclusive as to its efficacy for the treatment of OCD.[5]

Attention Deficit Hyperactivity Disorder (ADHD) is a common disorder that is estimated to impact about 10 percent of children (about 5.4 million in the United States) who are between four and seventeen years of age. Individuals with this disorder have been classified within one of the following categories: "hyperactive/impulsive subtype" (excessive movement, impetuous actions, frequent interruptions and inappropriate exclamations); "inattentive subtype" (absentmindedness, forgetfulness, disorganization); or "combined subtype" (combined manifestations of hyperactive/inattentive subtypes.) Individuals with ASD may demonstrate all of the symptoms of ADHD. ADHD has been reported to be the most frequent coexisting psychiatric disorder in children with ASD and the manifestations of these two disorders may frequently overlap. However, the ADHD inattentive subtype is significantly more frequent (65 percent according to one sample) with ASD, while neuro-typical individuals are more likely to manifest the combined ADHD subtype.[6]

Estimated rates of ADHD in individuals with ASD range from 30 to 50 percent. One study reported an ADHD rate of 55 percent when sub-threshold cases of ADHD were included.[7] Recently, researchers have reported that ADHD has specific and unique manifestations that are not inherent, and should not be considered as part of the ASD diagnosis. However, the combination of ADHD and ASD may predispose those individuals to additional psychiatric problems, since one study noted that nearly 85 percent of individuals with coinciding ASD/ADHD also were diagnosed with an additional psychological disorder.[8]

Although the core symptoms of this disorder usually start before twelve years of age, ADHD may be difficult to recognize in adults. ADHD rating scales, psychological tests, a careful childhood history and excluding other mental health disorders such as depression, anxiety, conduct disorders, learning and language deficits, or other psychiatric disorders are important considerations. Furthermore, other medical conditions such as seizure disorders, thyroid problems, sleep disorders, brain injury, or low blood sugar (hypoglycemia) should also be excluded. Medication side effects and/or substance abuse have also been misdiagnosed as ADHD.

The treatment of ADHD in adults is usually complex, requires careful monitoring, and frequently entails a period of prolonged adjustments and fine tuning. Therapy most often entails a combination of medication(s), education, skills training, and counseling. Medications are often the mainstay of therapy. Stimulants, which include substances such as methylphenidate or amphetamine, are typically the most commonly prescribed medications for ADHD. These types of medications appear to boost and balance levels of brain chemicals called neurotransmitters. Other medications used to treat ADHD include the non-stimulant atomoxetine; clonidine (which stimulates the alpha-adrenergic receptors in the brainstem and is also used to treat hypertension), and certain antidepressants such as bupropion.

Various forms of counseling are also recommended for the treatment of this disorder. These interventions, which may have very limited applicability for non-verbal and cognitively impaired individuals, include approaches such as:

1. Psychotherapy allows individuals with ADHD to talk about issues that bother them, explore negative behavior patterns, and learn ways to deal with their symptoms. According to the Mayo Clinic,[9] psychotherapy may provide the following benefits:
   a. Improve time management and organizational skills.
   b. Reduce your impulsive behavior.
   c. Develop better problem-solving skills.
   d. Cope with past academic, work, or social failures.
   e. Improve your self-esteem.
   f. Improve relationships with your family, co-workers, and friends.
   g. Develop strategies to control emotional outbursts and loss of temper.
2. Cognitive behavioral therapy teaches specific skills to manage and improve behavioral activities and changes negative thinking patterns into positive ones. It may enable ADHD individuals to improve their coping skills with employment challenges; enhance their relationship with coworkers; address other relationship problems; and help correct other conditions, such as depression or substance misuse.

Family therapy is a type of psychological counseling (psychotherapy) that can help family members improve communication and resolve conflicts. This form of therapy, which is often short term, may include family members, friends, and potentially even peers or coworkers who may also be dealing with issues related to ADHD. A distinctive component of this form of therapy is the potential to identify and correct specific family-based patterns of behaviors that may be contributing to the ADHD.

Anxiety disorder, an umbrella term that covers several different forms of a type of common psychiatric manifestation, has been reported to occur in over 40 percent of individuals with ASD. Typically an anxiety disorder is characterized by excessive rumination, worrying, uneasiness, apprehension, and fear about future uncertainties either based on real or imagined events, which may affect both physical and psychological health. Individuals with an anxiety disorder will suffer a fear and anticipate a terrifying consequence that is overwhelming and completely out of proportion to the actual potential danger. It is estimated that over 40 percent of individuals with ASD suffer from an anxiety disorder, which is much higher than the prevalence of anxiety disorders reported for the general population in America (18 percent) or in Europe (14 percent). Anxiety disorders have been further classified as "generalized anxiety disorder" (a long-lasting anxiety that is not focused on any one object or situation); "phobic disorder" (a fear and anxiety that is triggered by a specific stimulus or situation); and "panic disorder" (brief attacks of intense terror and apprehension that are associated with severe physical changes such as trembling, nausea, sweating, etc.).

Symptoms and manifestations of anxiety may include "physical reactions" (fatigue, difficulty with sleeping, heart-related symptoms, headaches, and evidence of adrenaline hyperactivity), "behavioral manifestations" (fidgeting, avoidance, distress manifestations), or "cognitive indications" (inattention, worrying, irritability). Specific phobias or fears have been reported in over 40 percent of individuals with ASD. The most common phobias in children with ASD have included fear of needles and/or injections, as well as fear of crowds. Over 10 percent of children with ASD have had a fear of loud noises, which is an uncommon phobia in typically developing children. About one-third of individuals with ASD have reported some degree of social anxiety such as the fear of being disliked or negatively evaluated in a social situation. About 10 percent of ASD populations have reported recurrent panic attacks that have not been associated with any specific stimuli or precipitating event.

Since virtually all of the manifestations of anxiety disorders may also be noted with ASD, differentiating these two conditions is extremely challenging. Noting a specific change in activities or behaviors in an individual with ASD may signal the onset of a concurrent anxiety disorder. For example, avoidance of previously tolerated tasks, resistance to usual routines, changes in frustration tolerances, increased ritualistic behaviors, and/or seeking repetitive reassurances may all signal the onset of an anxiety disorder concurrently with ASD. Many of the pharmacologic therapeutic agents, such as the selective serotonin reuptake inhibitors (SSRI) or the atypical antipsychotic agents, that are prescribed for anxiety disorders, have also been frequently administered for the treatment of ASD.

Major depressive disorder, or major depression, is a common psychiatric illness that is typically characterized by a combination of symptoms that include changes in mood and loss of interest and that interfere with a person's ability to function normally. Additional manifestations of major depressions may also include poor concentration, insomnia, fatigue, poor self-esteem, appetite disturbances, excessive guilt, and suicidal ideation. It is estimated that depression has an annual prevalence of about 10 percent of the general population in the United States and that about 17 percent of Americans will suffer at least one episode of this disorder during their lifetime. Although the vast majority of cases of depression are idiopathic (unknown causes), depression may also be a manifestation of an underlying medical condition such as hypothyroidism, multiple sclerosis, chronic pain syndrome, cerebrovascular disease, sleep apnea, anemia, diabetes, or cancer.

Depression has also been associated with ASD. For example, the original description of autism by Kanner included the tendency of some individuals to lapse into a "momentary fit of depression.[10] A study of sixty-four children and adolescents with ASD reported that depression was the most common psychiatric disorder, affecting about 2 percent of the sample population.[11] Depression has also been reported to be more common in children aged ten to twelve years old with high-functioning autism/Asperger syndrome than in the general population of the same age.[12]

Depression may occur more frequently in individuals with Asperger Syndrome and studies have reported the presence of depression in the range of 30–37 percent of adults with this disorder.[13] It is speculated that depression with Asperger Syndrome and high-functioning autism could be related to a greater awareness of their disability and progressive frustrations related to a sense of being different from their peer group and/or an inability to partake in social activities.

In individuals with ASD, the most common presenting symptoms of depression may be increased agitation, self-injurious behaviors, and/or temper tantrum outbursts. Other manifestations of depressions as a psychiatric comorbidity with ASD may include changes in sleep patterns, loss of interest in preferred activities, increase in stereotypical behaviors such as "hand-flapping," and/or decrease in the level of function or attention to tasks. Mania and hyperactivity have also been noted as atypical manifestations of depression in individuals with ASD or Asperger syndrome. Complications of depression and ASD have also included rare incidences of catatonia. Some researchers have also postulated that depression and ASD may be linked by genetic predisposition and family history.

NOTES

1. Psychiatric GWAS Consortium Coordinating Committee, Cichon S, Craddock N, Daly M, Faraone SV, Gejman PV, Kelsoe J, Lehner T, Levinson DF, Moran A, Sklar P, Sullivan PF, "Genomewide association studies: history, rationale, and prospects for psychiatric disorders," *Am J Psychiatry.* 2009 May;166(5):540–56.
2. Lai, Meng-Chuan et al., "Prevalence of co-occurring mental health diagnoses in the autism population: a systematic review and meta-analysis," *The Lancet Psychiatry*, Volume 6, Issue 10, 819 – 829.

3. Van Steensel FJA. et al. "Anxiety Disorders in Children and Adolescents with Autistic Spectrum Disorders: A Meta-Analysis," *Clinical Child & Family Psychology Review.* 2011: 14: 302–317.

4. Burchie, Hollander, Pallanti, "From treatment response to recovery: a realistic goal in OCD," *International Journal of Neuropsychopharmacology.* 2018;21(11):1007–1013. doi:10.1093/ijnp/pyy079.

5. Lefaucheur JP, André-Obadia N, Antal A, Ayache SS, Baeken C, Benninger DH, et al. (November 2014). "Evidence-based guidelines on the therapeutic use of repetitive transcranial magnetic stimulation (rTMS)." *Clinical Neurophysiology.* 125 (11): 2150–2206. doi:10.1016/j.clinph.2014.05.021. PMID 25034472. S2CID 206798663.

6. Gadow K. D., DeVincent C. J., Pomeroy J., "ADHD symptom subtypes in children with pervasive developmental disorder," J. Autism Dev. Disord. 36, 271–283 (2006).

7. Lefaucheur JP, André-Obadia N, Antal A, Ayache SS, Baeken C, Benninger DH, et al., "Evidence-based guidelines on the therapeutic use of repetitive transcranial magnetic stimulation (rTMS)," *Clinical Neurophysiology.* 125 (11): 2150–2206. November 2014.

8. Francisca J. A. van Steensel, Susan M. Bögels, Esther I. de Bruin, "Psychiatric Comorbidity in Children with Autism Spectrum Disorders: A Comparison with Children with ADHD," *J Child Fam Stud,* 22:368–376, 2013.

9. https//www.mayoclinic.org/testsprocedures/psychotherapy.

10. Kanner, L. "Autistic Disturbance Of Affective Contact," *Nervous Child,* 2:217–250. 1943.

11. Ghaziuddin et al. "Comorbidity of Autistic Disorder in Children and Adolescents," *European Child & Adolescent Psychiatry.* 1:209–213. 1992.

12. Kim, J. et al. "The prevalence of anxiety and mood problems amongst children with autism and Asperger syndrome," *Autism.* 4(2):117–132. (2000).

13. Wing, L. "Asperger's Syndrome, a clinical account," *Psychological Medicine,* 11:115–119. 1981; Ghaziuddin et al. "Depression in children with autism/pervasive developmental disorders: a case-control family history study," *Journal of Autism and Developmental Disorders.* 28:111–115 1998.

15

OLIVER SACKS' LOST BROTHER

Over a career of more than a half-century, neurologist and writer Oliver Sacks explored brain differences and disorders in thirteen major books and dozens of articles. He was responsible as much as anyone for introducing autism to a general audience in the 1990s. In a series of articles and the 1995 book, *An Anthropologist on Mars*, Sacks did one of the first public profiles of Temple Grandin, as well as of Stephen Wilshire, an autistic savant who could recreate entire cityscapes and skylines after one viewing. A theme throughout his articles and books: brain differences, even "defects, disorders and diseases," can bring out latent powers, and unusual skills and talents "that might never be seen, or ever be imaginable in their absence."[1]

Beyond his writing, achieving a world-wide readership, Sacks was also known as a clinician, treating brain disorders heretofore not successfully treated. His most well-known clinical cases involved post-encephalitic patients in New York and his use of the new drug levodopa in the early 1970s: cases which became the basis of his book *Awakenings*, later made into a movie.

But for all of Sacks' expertise, insight, and clinical ability, he was not able to help his younger brother Michael, with Michael's brain disorders and mental health conditions. Michael's story is introduced

153

in Sacks' 2001 book, *Uncle Tungsten*, and described in greater detail in Sacks' 2015 autobiography, *On the Move*. The story underscores several themes of the past few chapters: the value of having a job, the role of a support network, and also how difficult it can be to address certain mental health comorbidities.

Both Sacks' father and mother were prominent physicians and his two older brothers showed intellectual gifts at an early age (his brother Marcus spoke half a dozen languages by the age of sixteen), and later they too became physicians. Michael showed promise as a young man. Sacks describes him in his youth as "very intelligent; he read continually, had a prodigious memory."[2] Sacks adds that Michael in his youth was able to recite *Nicolas Nickleby* and *David Copperfield* by heart.

But at age fifteen, Michael began to show signs of schizophrenia, and he began a rapid descent into a world of delusion, anger, and recrimination.

"Torn between bliss and torment, fantasy and reality, feeling he was going mad (or perhaps so already), Michael could no longer sleep to rest, but agitatedly strode to and fro in the house, stamping his feet, glaring, hallucinating, shouting."

In 1944, at age sixteen, he was admitted to a psychiatric hospital and given insulin shock therapy, which seemed to halt the psychosis. But it did not "cure" the psychosis and Michael over the next years continued to be plagued by psychiatric episodes—"violently agitated, shouting, stamping, hallucinated" states. Sacks remarks of his own departure from England in July 1960: "When I left England on my twenty-seventh birthday, it was, among many other reasons, partly to get away from my tragic, hopeless, mismanaged brother."

Through a patient of his father, the owner of a large accounting business in London, Michael was able, at the age of seventeen, to find employment as a messenger delivering letters and packages throughout the city. In Sacks' view, the job provided structure, even purpose, to Michael. Michael saw himself as providing a valued service, and was scrupulous in delivering the material directly into the hands of the recipient.

In the early 1950s, when the first tranquilizers came into use, Michael's physician prescribed the tranquilizer Largactil to help control the hallucinations and delusions that had not ended. The psychotic episodes slowed, but according to Sacks also left Michael feeling dulled and muffled: "he had lost the sharpness and clarity with which he had previously perceived the world." Michael would tell Sacks, "It is like being softly killed."

After settling in America in 1960, Sacks had only sporadic contact with Michael, connecting mainly on family visits to London. Michael continued to work as a messenger, and live with his parents, but to Sacks on his visits, he seemed increasingly solitary, alone. "My father hoped that our synagogue might provide moral and pastoral support, a sense of community," but Michael, who once attended synagogue regularly and wore *tzitzit* and *teffalin*, the Jewish prayer garments, lost interest and the synagogue "lost interest in him."

In 1984, the firm employing Michael was sold and, after nearly thirty-five years as a messenger, his job was eliminated. According to Sacks, Michael tried to learn new skills, teaching himself typing, shorthand, and bookkeeping, but after several interviews, decided he would not be successful. He took up smoking and rarely ventured from the home: "He spent hours sitting in the lounge, smoking and staring into space; this is how I would usually find him when I visited London in the mid and later 1980s."

After their father died in 1990, the family sold the home, and Michael moved into a nearby residence in London for elderly Jewish people with mental illnesses. The family worried about the move, but Michael took it in stride and it brought him out of his isolation and he came to assume certain roles in his new community, in helping other residents with tasks such as laundry and, due to his lifetime of reading, becoming "a virtual encyclopedia whom the other residents could consult." He lived until 2006; his death was linked to his heavy smoking in later years.

Sacks does not seek to draw lessons from Michael's life—other than as one of the factors behind Sacks' own lifelong quest to understand brain disorders. But Sacks' telling does emphasize how stubborn comorbidities can be. The leading psychiatrists and pharmacologists in England were not able to effectively address Michael's psychosis.

At the same time, Michael's story does highlight the positive role of employment. Employment did not "solve" Michael's troubles, but his messenger job did play a number of positive roles. It was only when the job was eliminated that his isolation increased and his health declined. Later, at the Jewish home for the aged, he became less isolated as he found other services he could provide, even if non-paid.

Further, Michael both benefited from having a family support network, and might have benefited more if Sacks and his brothers had been more involved. The family was able to provide him with access to mental health professionals, a secure home, and helped him get his messenger job. But at least according to Sacks' account, the family's involvement in finding new social networks for Michael dimmed over time, and family members did not actively step in when he lost his messenger job in 1984 and was searching for a new career. Reflecting on his own behavior even before he left England, Sacks writes:

> I could, I should, have been more loving, more supportive, while I was back in London, in medical school; I could have gone out with Michael to restaurants, films, theatres, concerts; I could have gone with him on visits to the seaside or the countryside. But I didn't; and the shame of this—the feeling that I was a bad brother, not available to him when he was in such need—is still hot within me sixty years later.

NOTES

1. Oliver Sacks, *An Anthropologist on Mars*, New York, Alfred Knopf, 1995.
2. Oliver Sacks, *On the Move*, New York, Vintage Books, 2015.

16

WHAT OF ADULTS WITH AUTISM WITHOUT SUPPORT NETWORKS?

A main theme of this volume is the role of support networks, primarily family members of adults with autism, in finding jobs. The support networks help carve out opportunities for internships, work experience or jobs. They are there to mediate for work problems that arise.

But what of adults with autism without these support networks? What of adults, especially young adults, who do not have family members who are able to assist in the job process? It's a question that we at AASCEND have discussed often over the past few years.

Some of these adults without support networks will be fine in the job world; they are able to make their own way. They possess executive skills in identifying resources and pursuing them, and do not have the more serious neurological or mental health obstacles to fitting into the workplace.

For the others, the community groups do provide job search and job placement assistance, as we have seen. But one needs to know how to access this assistance; and the assistance has limits. These community groups rarely can provide the required intensive and on-going assistance in locating jobs and meeting all of the job requirements, including administrative requirements.

For example, a young man we know with a significant learning disability was referred to an interview last month for a position at an Amazon distribution center. When he got there, he learned that he couldn't be interviewed because he didn't have a passport or birth certificate/and SSN. He has no idea how to obtain any of the documents and no family members to help. Staff at the community group referring him, with sizable case loads, didn't have the bandwidth on this time-consuming administrative detail. The document search may be resolved soon. But it is the annoying administrative details, calling on absent executive functions, that often sink job searches.

Mutual support groups like AASCEND can fill in the gaps, but only to an extent. Camilla Bixler, our AASCEND co-chair, has taken it upon herself to do so for years; helping with connections to emergency housing, or SSI application, or interactions with law enforcement. But she can only do so much. These interactions with bureaucracies require multiple phone calls and follow up, and are rarely resolved easily.

Religious orders in the past have stepped in to provide the family role and support network for adults with developmental or mental health conditions. In *Brideshead Revisited*, Sebastian is taken in by the Catholic monks in Morocco. They give him odd jobs at the hospital they operate, care for him on a daily basis, and accept him without reservation. "I've seen others like him, and I believe they are very near and dear to God," his sister Cordelia explains, adding that she sees her brother as a "great favorite with the old fathers."[1]

But monasteries and convents are scarce today. The major churches, synagogues, and mosques, who say they care for the dispossessed, offer no support networks to replace a missing family network. Nor do the foundations or other major non-profits.

That's why today we may see some of these adults without support networks on a daily basis. They are men and women who are outside of the job world. We may see them talking or laughing to themselves on street corners. They may live in group homes or single occupancy hotels or at no stable address, but they are not far from homelessness. They often don't have the executive functions not only needed in a job search, but also to even get government benefits they may be entitled to.

It may be that there are no better alternatives for support structures in our large, secular, complex society. This, though, remains a big challenge for autism employment advocates and a big gap that no government program can fill.

NOTE

1. Evelyn Waugh, *Brideshead Revisited,* Boston, Little, Brown and Company, 1945.

17

OUR INDIVIDUAL JOB JOURNEYS IN 2021 AND BEYOND

No government Act or program can guarantee a role in the job world for adults with autism. They and their support networks must do it themselves, through their own employment journeys. The Act's role will be to assist, not replace, these journeys.

Part I: Why Adults with Autism Must Carve Out Their Own Job Roles

An Autism Full Employment Act will not solve the employment challenges of Lou's son, Mark, or my son William, or most of our other AASCEND members. These challenges are complex and will likely continue throughout their lifetimes. In the end, our sons and daughters must solve these challenges themselves, with our help and with the help of the broader autism community.

Their success will be based on their ability to find or carve out a niche in the job market for themselves. No government program can do this, for any worker. They and their support network must undertake their own journeys, to find a role in which they add value to an enterprise and serve others.

Lou has described the job journey of Mark in chapter 13. Let me now add a word on the job journey of William in the past few years.

I wrote in 2015 in *The Autism Job Club* about William's rocky job search in the first three years following his graduation from Cal State University East Bay. He participated in internship programs with the County of Alameda and with the large utility, Pacific Gas & Electric, but neither led to a regular job with these companies. At the time of writing that book, he was starting a position in data entry with the law firm of Holland & Knight.

That position lasted a year, before it ended in 2016. Since then, William has been employed in a series of jobs, but he has yet to find his niche. He has had fourteen jobs during this time; some short-term by intention, others ending due to William's behaviors and inability to fit into the workplace.

William is preternaturally upbeat and positive, and employers and coworkers like this. However, William also has behaviors that employers and co-workers find disconcerting: he loudly talks to himself and laughs to himself, often walks around with a Starbucks bag and old coffee cups and plastic forks, makes a mess in the lunchroom, and has a compulsion to hide old food in various locations. He has little understanding of money or any ability to manage it. If you asked him to write out a check to you for five thousand dollars, he'd do it (he's done it before).

He retains some of the prodigious memory skills from his childhood,[1] but has not found any real use for them in the job world. He has "time management" issues and arrives late most of the time (though usually only by a few minutes). Despite being in dozens of job search workshops over the past ten years, he has not been able to master the job search skills or websites, or update his profile on LinkedIn.

He wants a job as much as anyone I know. He takes great pride in having a workplace to go to. He takes comfort in the structure a job brings.

One of the targets of our job searches has been at entry level civil service jobs, with steady pay and a high degree of security (and direct deposit). He has applied for twenty-two City/County of San Francisco positions and eighteen California state government positions (mainly office tech). He has gotten three interviews, but has never come close.

Prior to the pandemic, he had a provisional position at a local government department, but that failed to turn into an on-going position. During the pandemic he's been working half time at the Goodwill store on Fillmore Street, and half time at Code Tenderloin, a job training program near Market Street.

So he continues his journey, to find where he can contribute, what he is good at, and what his niche is. It may be in some form of office administration, or it may be in customer relations, or working with seniors, or in a field we haven't thought of yet.

His journey is now nearly seven years old. I know it might take another seven years or more. At the same time, I've learned that job lives are highly unpredictable. Sometimes a niche is found when and where least expected if you keep up an active job search.

While his niche is unclear, what is clear is the type of workplace that will allow him and many other adults with autism to find their role. To recall from chapter 6, it is a workplace in which adults with autism do not need to be worried daily about being fired for odd or inappropriate behaviors. It is a workplace with patience and as much flexibility as possible. It is a workplace that doesn't overlook the positives that adults with autism often bring to the workplace in their desire for and appreciation of their jobs. It is a workforce with managers who welcome adults with autism.

The novels of Charles Dickens contain a series of characters who provide a kindly, nonjudgmental, and supportive environment for others, often coming from dark or chaotic situations: Joe Gargery in *Great Expectations*, Noddy Boffin in *Our Mutual Friend*, and Aunt Betsey Trotwood in *David Copperfield*, to name a few. Betsey Trotwood takes in young David and protects him from the Murdstones. She also has taken in Richard Babley ("Mr. Dick"), with his childlike characteristics and obsessions. She appreciates Babley for his basic goodness and does not judge him—one academic dissertation identifies Babley as being on the autism spectrum.[2] I want a workplace manager like Betsey Trotwood for all of our AASCEND members.

Finding these managers and building these "autism friendly" workplaces will call forth individual and collective efforts among adults with autism and family members. In the short term, William and other adults with autism and their support teams need to seek out existing autism-friendly workplaces with managers like Betsey Trotwood. At the same time, it is up to the autism community to build autism-friendly workplaces far more widely. This effort will enlist the resources of the autism workforce consultancies, national autism agencies, and local autism employment providers, joining with national and state human resource associations and trade associations.

In his magisterial *Wealth and Poverty*, George Gilder quotes the twentieth-century Spanish philosopher Jose Ortega y Gasset, "All life is the struggle, the effort to be itself. The difficulties which I meet with in order to realize my existence are precisely what awaken and mobilize my activities, my capacities." And Gilder adds, "A guaranteed job denies the crucial fact that all jobs are to some extent created by the worker; it is only he who can guarantee the job, by the act of supplying labor, undergoing hardship, achieving distinction, and thus becoming part of the struggle by which human life improves itself."[3]

This idea of moral agency through job search and retention may seem far too metaphysical for an autism population that has such difficulty finding and holding employment. But it is true for the autism workforce, as with the broader workforce. "Whether I shall turn out to be the hero of my own life, or whether that station will be held by anybody else, these pages must show," is the opening line of *David Copperfield*, indicating David's ability to determine his station and role. Both the ability to determine a job future and the challenge to do so is not to be ignored in autism employment.

Even if government could somehow "guarantee" a job, in nearly all cases, we would not want to eliminate the journey. With all of the failures, disappointments, and unhappiness in William's job journey over the past seven years, I would not see it replaced for him by a government guaranteed income or guaranteed job. I know William wouldn't. It's his journey.

Part II: How the Act Can Assist Their Journeys

What the Act and government can do is assist the journeys of adults with autism and other developmental differences. The strategies set out in this volume are starting points for building this assistance.

Since adults with autism are so diverse, so too is the diversity of strategies. They are mainly market-oriented, focused on competitive employment, but with allowance for public service employment and new forms of congregate workplaces for the most severely impacted. They build in mutual support and self-help by the autism community. They aim for true autism-friendly workplaces, far beyond the physical accommodations of lighting, noise reduction, or quiet rooms.

To briefly review, among private businesses, the main venue in autism employment has been large companies, implementing targeted autism employment programs. In nearly all cases, these are proving effective, as they accompany hiring with retention strategies. The Act will further their expansion across industries and sectors, through several strategies, a chief one of which will be the emerging subindustry of workforce consultancies.

These consultancies, often staffed by persons with ties to the autism community and experience in the business world, are providing customized recruitment, hiring, job coaching and retention services today to some of the large companies. They are clear-eyed about the challenges, and able to see past much of the magical thinking that can permeate autism employment. They can reach many more businesses, as they can expand their efforts.

Additionally, these workforce consultancies represent a mechanism to engage midsize and small firms in autism employment. Up to now these firms haven't been much engaged, lacking expertise and resources. With some level of public funding, they are able to provide services, at no cost, to small and midsize businesses—which will be necessary, at least in the near future.

The universities and large non-profits are a natural setting for the autism-friendly workplace, given their missions, generally relaxed environments, and absence of the financial pressures present in businesses. In *Exiting Nirvana*, Claire Claiborne Park describes the long-time employment of her daughter, Jessy, a person with autism, in the mailroom at Williams College. Jessy has found her employment niche, which provides her with a steady job while she pursues her avocation as a painter. The mailroom is only one option. Universities have dozens of other occupations in instruction, administration, and operations. Universities should be expected to do much more in this hiring—especially those receiving autism research funds. Similarly with the large non-profits, they are natural settings for employing adults with autism and being true autism-friendly workplaces.

State and local governments are also natural settings for increased autism employment and true autism-friendly workplaces. These governments only need to implement the same hiring and retention models for autism hiring that they are urging private sector employers to follow. The autism-focused businesses put into practice the culture of autism-friendly workplaces and real jobs. They both provide employment to those unable to find jobs in other settings and turn out a product or service in demand. As we have seen, these businesses are very limited in size, require extraordinary commitments by their entrepreneurs, and exist financially on the razor's edge. The Act will bolster their financial viability. It will give attention to those autism-focused businesses that hire the more severely-impacted adults, and will look at other strategies for these often-forgotten adults.

Part III. Tocqueville's Heirs

Mutual support runs throughout all of the strategies put forward in the previous chapters. It includes mutual support among adults with autism and family members in job searching (autism job clubs), in advocacy for an autism employment effort within their worksites, and in supporting autism-focused businesses. It includes advocacy for state and local government hiring and job creation for the more severely impacted.

This past weekend we taped a new edition of "Life on the Autism Spectrum," the television show that AASCEND has produced since 2016. Our guests were Cathy and Jim Gott ("Autism Meets the Gotts and the Major Leagues").

Jim pitched in the major leagues for fourteen years, with the Toronto Blue Jays, San Francisco Giants, and Los Angeles Dodgers, and currently is bullpen coach for the Philadelphia Phillies. He and his wife Cathy have two sons with autism, CJ, thirty-two, and Danny, twenty-seven.

Jim talked on the show about how much autism is now part of the consciousness of Major League Baseball: "Autism Awareness Day is now league-wide, with all thirty-two teams. With the Phillies, I hear from everyone from groundskeepers to the front office, of their connections to autism, someone has a son or grandson or nephew, and they want to help."

Most of the show focused on Cathy's efforts. Cathy has developed a series of autism education and employment projects over the past twenty-five years. "All of my projects grow out of problems I had in navigating the autism services, first the education system and later the social welfare system," she said. Her first project was Education Spectrum in 1996: "When I went to choose a school for Danny I found a confusing mix of regulations and requirement, so once I figured it out, I started Education Spectrum to help other parents navigate the process."

Next in 2007, came Danny's Farm: "When it came time to look at transition from high school, again I found no clear directions;

167

Danny's Farm is a petting zoo we created that provides work experience for youth with autism." In 2012, Cathy Gott helped start "Transitions," which connects parents with specialists in autism transition: "The disability system would hand out checklists and guidebooks on what to do, but these were not helpful; parents need individual assistance."

Currently, Cathy is engaged in her most ambitious effort: a series of housing developments providing housing for adults with autism in urban settings and mixed with "neuro-typical" adults. The first, "The Village" in the Pico-Robertson section of Los Angeles, is sixty-four units, and is expected to be completed in 2023.

Cathy has undertaken all of these projects without the benefit of a government or non-profit position, or foundation largesse, but as her own entrepreneur. All of the projects represent mutual support and self-help, by Cathy and other family members, advocates and adults with autism, who have not waited on the government to do something. "I know how much my family benefits from the efforts of previous generations in California—Frank Lanterman and others—in building the current disability system," Cathy said.

The Gotts and their colleagues, of course, are not alone in their extra-governmental efforts. Thousands of autism advocates across the nation are engaged in their own local efforts not only in employment, but also in autism housing developments, autism police relations, and autism mental health. They are part of the deep tradition in America of voluntary associations, Tocqueville's heirs.

***

IN THE EARLY years OF AASCEND, before autism became so prominent in the national consciousness, we thought of ourselves as part of another deep tradition in America, the venture into an unexplored wilderness. By the late 1990s, when AASCEND was founded, programs were being developed and tested for children and youth with autism. However, adults with autism largely were out of view, with little said about integration in employment and society.

The past two decades have brought an outpouring of activity in autism employment, and independent living. Yet, much of the wilderness for adults with autism remains.

A part of this wilderness involves the neurobiology of autism, and how some of the comorbidities that undermine employment and independent living can be addressed, as discussed in the previous chapter. The understanding of the brain wiring of autism and comorbidities has grown, but still little is known of how the wiring might be altered for mental health—and about alternatives to the medications that are so often prescribed today.

Other parts of the wilderness involve the many unknowns alluded to in the previous chapters, including how to scale the current successful employment efforts, how to involve the more severely impacted, and how workplaces might balance business imperatives and flexibility. There is still much to be learned even in the basic autism statistics and dynamics of who is employed, and in what types of employment, and for how long.

To adults with autism, family members, and advocates, come join us in our wilderness trek, our collective journey to move to the next stage of jobs for adults with autism and other learning and mental health differences. There is no formal membership required or diagnosis of autism or family relationship. Political party, race, and ethnicity mean nothing. We are of all views and races. Anyone who considers themselves part of the autism community is welcome.

We are united in what we agree on, that employment is central to our personal wellness and stability as a society. That's as true for adults with autism as for everyone else—probably more so.

NOTES

1. As described in *The Autism Job Club*, William from a young age on has had the ability to watch a television show one time and recite it word for word, to remember dates from a decade or earlier, and to recall events in great detail.

2. Penny Gill, "The Autistic Mr. Dick of David Copperfield," McGill University, Toronto, unpublished dissertation, May 2004.

3. George Gilder, *Wealth and Poverty*, New York, Bantam Books, 1981.

EPILOGUE

YOUR ROLE IN AUTISM EMPLOYMENT

How can you contribute to the Autism Full Employment Act? To autism fuller employment? To fuller employment among the range of adults with developmental differences?

Starting with the Act, we at AASCEND have formed a loose Autism Full Employment Coalition to draw together the people who have contacted us so far after hearing of the Act. We are reaching out to other autism groups around the country as well as to the autism and disability advocacy organizations in Washington, DC. We welcome hearing from you, either directly to Dr. Vismara and me or to our AASCEND website, info@aascend.org.

We know that passing the Act—or individual strategies in it—will be a process over the next few years. However, it is now clear that the Recovery itself will be a multi-year process, and the Recovery legislation will also be over a period of time—not a sprint in the first hundred days of the Biden Administration.

Dr. Vismara in particular has experience in autism legislation that takes years to enact, and in autism institutions that take years to build. In 2005, Dr. Vismara was one of the first advocates for an autism-related legislative effort in California State government. At the time, insurers in the state did not provide insurance coverage for most behavioral and mental health services for youth and adults with autism.

He joined with others in meeting with legislators and legislative staff, bringing together a coalition of persons with autism, family members, and mental health researchers. Several bills were introduced over a five year period that were either not enacted or rejected by the governors at the time. It was only in 2011 that SB946 was passed by the legislature and signed by Governor Jerry Brown. The bill required that insurers cover certain behavioral and mental health services, prescribed by health care professionals. Now it is accepted practice in California.

Dr. Vismara's background also involves bringing together autism coalitions and research professionals as one of the founders of the University of California, Davis MIND Institute. The Institute was established in the late 1990s to study the neurobiology of autism. Vismara started his efforts in 1995, after discovering the limited research budgets nationwide on the brain pathology of autism. At the time he had his cardiology practice, and recalls:

As a cardiologist I had witnessed amazing and impressive advances in the treatment of heart disease during the prior two decades. These improvements and breakthroughs had been achieved through rigorous scientific studies, which were well planned, coordinated, and adequately funded in excellent medical and research centers. We needed to implement the same approach for Autism Spectrum Disorder.

Building the conceptual framework for the Institute and fundraising took several years, but the MIND Institute was established, combining research with diagnosis, treatment, and parent education. Today it has a research budget of over thirty million dollars annually, drawing on faculty from sixteen UC Davis departments and schools. It has grown to include genomic medicine physicians, psychiatrists, developmental behavioral pediatricians, clinical psychologists, and genetic counselors, and, in 2017, had over six thousand patient visits.

In advancing the Act, we will utilize the techniques that Dr. Vismara utilized in his efforts: the coalition of persons with autism, family, and professionals, the flexibility to incorporate different views, and the combination of extra-governmental social capital/financial capital with public investment. Since AASCEND is a local group, we know we need one or more of the Washington, DC-based advocacy groups to assume a major role.

A national Act will provide resources for building a better system of autism employment and raising the profile of mutual support and self-help efforts for a better system. But this better system also will be built on thousands of other efforts on the local and community level. That's where most of us will have impact.

In this volume, we have set out multiple ways for persons with autism, family members, and advocates to become involved. To review five of the main ones:

- Advocacy within your workplace for fuller hiring and retention of adults with autism and other developmental differences. This workplace may be a private business or it may be an educational institution, nonprofit, or state or local government.
- Advocacy among the educational institutions, major nonprofits, and local government in your community for fuller hiring and retention of adults with autism and other developmental differences. These institutions have stated missions to do so, that they are not fulfilling.
- Support for the autism focused businesses, utilizing their products or services whenever possible.
- Becoming active in mutual support job clubs.
- Serving as a volunteer job coach or mentor.

Citizen autism groups like AASCEND exist throughout the United States. They, like AASCEND, are taking action in each of these five ways, and finding they can have impact.

When William and I first wandered into an AASCEND meeting in the summer of 2011, we knew little of the organization and none of the other members. Within a short time, though, it was clear we were among persons with autism and family members who "got it," who required no explanations, and for whom employment was a given. "After many years of searching, we're finally home," I thought then and have continued to think since. You will too, as you join the autism employment campaign.

ABOUT THE AUTHORS

Michael Bernick is a graduate of Harvard College, Oxford University (Balliol College), and the University of California, Berkeley School of Law. He has been involved in the employment field since 1979, including five years as director of California's state labor department, the Employment Development Department. Bernick is the author of five previous books, including *The Autism Job Club* (2015). He is currently employment law counsel with the international law firm of Duane Morris LLP, as well as a fellow at the Milken Institute and adjunct faculty at Stanford Medical School.

Louis A. Vismara, MD is the parent of four children, including his son, Mark, who was diagnosed with autism in 1995. Vismara is the co-founder of the UC Davis MIND Institute, a founding member of the California's First Five Commission, and the California Legislative Blue Ribbon Commission on Autism. He is the recipient of numerous advocacy awards and was honored by the California Senate for his "lifetime achievements and meritorious service to humanity and the people of California." He is an advisor of the Stanford Neurodiversity Project and adjunct faculty professor at Stanford Medical School.

ACKNOWLEDGMENTS

Our editor, Caroline Russomanno, skillfully guided this volume, through several rewrites and edits. We want to start by thanking her, as well as our publisher, Tony Lyons. Both are deeply committed to improving the economic and social opportunities for adults with autism and other developmental differences.

Most of the persons who contributed to the employment strategies and ideas set forward in this book are included in the previous pages. Additionally, we'd like to acknowledge the following for their contributions:

Angelo K. Tsakopoulos and Chrysa Tsakopoulos Demos, who have championed the employment of adults with autism and other developmental differences through their numerous business and philanthropic ventures over many years.

Darrell Steinberg, Don Perata, and John Burton, California State Senate Presidents since 2000, who have advanced autism employment initiatives through state legislation.

Stephen H. Sutro, managing partner of the San Francisco office of Duane Morris LLP, for his on-going encouragement of this book project.

Eve Klein, Linda Hollinshead and Jim Brown of the Duane Morris employment and labor law group, who developed the Duane Morris webinar on legal guidelines, "Establishing an Effective Neurodiversity Hiring Program," and provided ongoing consultation on initiatives with private sector employers.

Dr. Lawrence Fung of the Stanford Neurodiversity Project, a project we are senior advisors to, combining research with direct assistance to job seekers.

Dr. Bryna Siegel, David Platzer, John Colburn, Hackie Reitman, Doug Meeker, David Van Etten, Marilyn Ridgway, Barbara Devaney, Valerie Baadh, and Helen Chan, for their editorial suggestions.

Bob Lanter and Brandon Anderson of the California Workforce Association, and Michelle O'Camb of the Sacramento Employment and Training Administration for their ideas on the role of Local Workforce Boards in autism employment.

Greg Yates and Camilla Bixler, The AASCEND Co-Chairs, for their support of the Autism Job Club, now in its tenth year, and our other AASCEND job placement activities.

Joan Schmidt and Tyrone Huddleston of Creative Living Options who provide employment services to the more severely impacted adults with autism, and have shared their ideas for increasing employment among this group.

Sheri Peifer and Darlene Cullivan of Eskaton Senior Care Services, who have partnered on a project employing adults with autism, including persons severely impacted, in assisted living and long term care facilities.

INDEX

OTHER BOOKS
BY MICHAEL BERNICK

The Dreams of Jobs (1984)
Urban Illusions (1987)
Transit Villages in the 21st Century (1996)
Job Training that Gets Results (2005)
The Autism Job Club (2015)